ALSO BY KELLI AND PETER BRONSKI

Artisanal Gluten-Free Cooking (Second Edition)
Gluten-Free Family Favorites
Artisanal Gluten-Free Cupcakes

ALSO BY PETER BRONSKI

The Gluten-Free Edge
(with Melissa McLean Jory, MNT)

No Gluten, No Problem

PIZZA

75+ RECIPES FOR EVERY CRAVING—FROM
THIN CRUST TO DEEP DISH, NEW YORK TO NAPLES

Kelli and Peter Bronski

PHOTOGRAPHY BY JENNIFER OLSON

THE EXPERIMENT

NEW YORK

No Gluten, No Problem Pizza: *75+ Recipes for Every Craving—from Thin Crust to Deep Dish, New York to Naples*
All text, and photographs on pages xiv–xix, 114–15, 118–19, 120–21, 182–83, 184–85, and 220, copyright © 2019
    by Kelli Bronski and Peter Bronski
Additional photographs copyright © 2019 by Jennifer Olson Photography

The Experiment, LLC
220 East 23rd Street, Suite 600
New York, NY 10010-4658
theexperimentpublishing.com

This book contains the opinions and ideas of its author. It is intended to provide helpful and informative material on the subjects addressed in the book. It is sold with the understanding that the author and publisher are not engaged in rendering medical, health, or any other kind of personal professional services in the book. The author and publisher specifically disclaim all responsibility for any liability, loss, or risk—personal or otherwise—that is incurred as a consequence, directly or indirectly, of the use and application of any of the contents of this book.

THE EXPERIMENT and its colophon are registered trademarks of The Experiment, LLC. Many of the designations used by manufacturers and sellers to distinguish their products are claimed as trademarks. Where those designations appear in this book and The Experiment was aware of a trademark claim, the designations have been capitalized.

The Experiment's books are available at special discounts when purchased in bulk for premiums and sales promotions as well as for fund-raising or educational use. For details, contact us at info@theexperimentpublishing.com.

Library of Congress Cataloging-in-Publication Data

Names: Bronski, Kelli, author. | Bronski, Peter, author.
Title: No gluten, no problem pizza : 75+ recipes for every craving-from
    thin crust to deep dish, New York to Naples / Kelli Bronski, Peter
    Bronski.
Description: New York : The Experiment, 2019. | Includes index.
Identifiers: LCCN 2019024418 (print) | LCCN 2019024419 (ebook) | ISBN
    9781615195411 | ISBN 9781615195428 (ebook)
Subjects: LCSH: Gluten-free diet--Recipes. | Food allergy--Diet
    therapy--Recipes. | LCGFT: Cookbooks.
Classification: LCC RM237.86 .B7524 2019 (print) | LCC RM237.86 (ebook) |
    DDC 641.5/639311--dc23
LC record available at https://lccn.loc.gov/2019024418
LC ebook record available at https://lccn.loc.gov/2019024419

ISBN 978-1-61519-541-1
Ebook ISBN 978-1-61519-542-8

Cover and text design by Beth Bugler
Cover photographs by Jennifer Olson Photography

Manufactured in China

First printing October 2019
10 9 8 7 6 5 4 3 2 1

TO ALL GLUTEN-FREE PIZZA
LOVERS WHO'VE BEEN MISSING
TRULY GREAT PIZZA

Contents

The Recipes

Reputations can be hard to shake. And let's be honest: Gluten-free pizza has a bad reputation. Yes, if you know where to look, you can snag some genuinely good gluten-free pizza. But that's the exception rather than the norm. The unfortunate reality is that there's a lot of mediocre gluten-free pizza out there. There's also some truly terrible gluten-free pizza.

Kelli and I are on a mission to change this reputation . . . *and* the reality behind it. Whether you have celiac disease, gluten sensitivity, a wheat allergy, or another reason for joining the gluten-free community—or you know someone who's part of it—you deserve truly great gluten-free pizza.

Let's launch a gluten-free pizza revolution, right in your very own kitchen.

The Problem with Most Gluten-Free Pizza

If you've had gluten-free pizza before, this tragedy is probably already familiar to you. It doesn't matter if you bought a premade crust from the frozen foods section of your supermarket or a pie from a pizzeria that outsources their gluten-free crusts from a third party, or if you've tried to make pizza at home with recipes that promise

What's the problem? Quite a bit, actually. For starters, almost all gluten-free pizza crusts fall into a single style: ultrathin. These superthin crusts become hard like a cracker once baked, and their flavor is often bland and overly starchy. They're also tiny—ten inches (twenty-five centimeters) is a common diameter. And they're expensive, often commanding a hefty gluten-free surcharge at many pizzerias and a price premium at the supermarket.

Upholding Tradition: Why This Matters to Us

Listen, we're not here to pick a fight with bad gluten-free pizza (though it sorta has it comin'). And we're not here to point fingers at specific companies, especially those well-intentioned companies that are bringing safe gluten-free foods to market for the celiac and broader gluten-free community.

We're here to provide a solution to a long-standing problem. Because for us, pizza is a passion.

We're both from New York, where the thread of pizza pride runs strong. My maternal grandfather's family emigrated from Sicily in the early twentieth century. From the tenements in lower Manhattan, they migrated east to Brooklyn and Queens, and eventually to Long Island, where I was born and raised. With this family heritage and regional upbringing, our love of pizza is genetically ingrained.

After Kelli and I got married in 2003, we adopted her family tradition and made it our own: weekly pizzas every Sunday night. We'd roll up our sleeves and make a floury mess in the kitchen together as a couple before sitting down to enjoy a freshly baked homemade pizza.

In the years since, as our three children have come into the family picture, the tradition has continued, evolving and growing along with our family. Now, there are more floury hands in the kitchen. We've added a soundtrack to the evening, heavily populated with Italian American and Italian crooners like Lou Monte, Connie Francis, Jerry Vale, and others, whose music reminds me of visiting my grandparents in my childhood. There's also Italian red wine, usually Valpolicella or nebbiolo, for Kelli and me and nonalcoholic almond or cherry Italian sodas for the kids. Of course, the center of the tradition is the pizza itself.

But more than twelve years ago, this pizza tradition was thrown for a major loop when I was diagnosed with celiac disease and we converted our household to be gluten-free.

A Celiac Disease Diagnosis and Early Experiences with Gluten-Free Pizza

My celiac diagnosis came after years of sickness. Once I adopted a strict gluten-free diet, my health rebounded impressively. But make no mistake: Adopting a gluten-free diet came with a steep learning curve, numerous baking false starts, and one particular pizza tragedy-meets-comedy.

In those first weeks and months of going gluten-free more than a dozen years ago—me for medical reasons and Kelli in solidarity—we were gluten-free-pizza newbies. But we desperately wanted to continue our weekly Sunday night pizza-making tradition. We weren't willing to lose it.

Thinking that a gluten-free-pizza mix from the supermarket would be a fast path to success, we bought one made by a company that shall forever remain nameless. Following our then-typical division of kitchen labor, Kelli prepared the dough, which I'd then shape, top, and launch in the oven.

"The pizza dough is ready for you," she called over.

Peering into the mixing bowl, I saw a batter that—to my great surprise—had the look and consistency of cake frosting. "How am I supposed to shape that into a pizza?" I asked incredulously.

At Pizzeria Focacceria Quattrocento in northern Italy, with two-time World Pizza Championship gluten-free division winner, Federico De Silvestri, and his wife, Mara

"You're not. You pour it into a pan and spread it with a spatula."

The Sicilian American New Yorker in me recoiled in horror. But we kept the faith and dutifully baked the pizza, only to have our hopes and dreams shattered. The crust puffed to twice the height of a slice of thick Sicilian pizza, and the crumb had the texture of sponge cake. It may have been topped with tomato sauce and mozzarella cheese, but this was *not* pizza. At least not by our standards.

We needed to find a better way.

The No Gluten, No Problem Journey

For us, "finding a better way" first involved months of testing to develop what became our signature all-purpose gluten-free flour blend. The recipe is published prominently on our website and it's in every cookbook we've written (except for this book, which doesn't use the blend for reasons we'll explain). It has been the bedrock of most of our gluten-free baking.

As we surmounted the gluten-free learning curve and started converting old recipes and developing new ones, we wanted to help others in the gluten-free community get to the other side of their own journey to becoming gluten-free.

In 2008 we launched our website, No Gluten, No Problem. A series of cookbooks followed, including what has become our flagship: *Artisanal Gluten-Free Cooking*. First released in 2009, it was revised and updated a few years later and remains popular today.

As the 2000s gave way to the 2010s, many gluten-free foods made significant strides in taste, texture, and nutrition. Recipes were getting better (including ours). A number of excellent dedicated gluten-free bakeries sprung up in gluten-free hot spots around the country.

Yet, for some reason, gluten-free pizza seemed to have been left behind. Sure, gluten-free pizza *sales* were growing, but the pizza itself wasn't improving. We knew it could be better—much better. The pathway, we believed, was not through better premade frozen crusts but rather through recipes and the home gluten-free cooks—like you and us—who'd make them.

Moreover, we wanted to create recipes that weren't just *different* from what we'd done previously but that would make our own previously published recipes *obsolete*. (We dare say that we've succeeded, and then some. Though you be the judge!) With a respect for pizza tradition, we set out to create gluten-free pizzas that are as authentic as possible to the tastes and textures of their respective styles. From New York to Neapolitan and beyond, the pizzas should look, feel, and taste like their original gluten-filled counterparts.

Thus began a year of intensive recipe development and testing, with a special "field trip" thrown in during the process.

From Colorado to Italy to New York and Back

Before we got too deep into gluten-free pizza recipe development, we first needed to do some serious pizza research. We'd heard through the gluten-free grapevine that a small handful of pizzerias—some in New York, many more in Italy, and a few others scattered across the United States, Europe, and Australia—were doing impressive things with gluten-free pizza.

Pizzaiolo Angelo Caprio at Pizzeria Mascagni in Naples, Italy

These pizzerias were in a class of their own: They made their own gluten-free pizza dough in house from scratch, either starting with a blend or concocting their own. They had dedicated gluten-free ingredient stations. Dedicated gluten-free pizza ovens. Dedicated gluten-free kitchens. And in two cases, entire gluten-free pizzerias.

Naturally, we needed to taste these pizzas and meet the pizza makers! And, if they'd let us, step into their kitchens and learn how they did it and with what ingredients. What we found among those pizzaioli and their pizzerias was incredible generosity and openness—and a strong source of inspiration and motivation.

In early summer 2018, we packed up our three kids and hit the road, first to Italy. We began in the north, visiting pizzerias in and around Milan, Bergamo, and Verona. From there, we drove south through Tuscany and into the heart of Rome. And finally, farther south still to the Campania region, the birthplace of pizza, and cities such as Naples, Sorrento, and Salerno. We then packed our bags, reluctantly said goodbye to Italy, and flew to New York City, where more pizzerias dotted our itinerary. (They are too numerous to name individually here, but many are mentioned in the headnotes of our recipes, and we encourage you to check out the full list in the acknowledgments at the end of the book.)

Our gluten-free pizza global adventure involved more than 1,500 miles of driving, visiting nearly twenty-five pizzerias and eating more than sixty gluten-free pizzas. (I didn't get sick from gluten cross-contamination even once.)

Our Year of Gluten-Free Pizza

And then our family's Year of Gluten-Free Pizza really began. Day after day, the pizzas kept coming, and coming, and coming. We combined what we'd learned from our travels in Italy and New York with our dozen years of experience in gluten-free baking and recipe development, holding ourselves—and our pizzas—to an uncompromisingly high standard.

The hardest part was developing the doughs themselves. But this was the most important work. Some people see a pizza's crust merely as a delivery mechanism for the toppings. But we believe the crust itself matters, too. And if you've ever had a bad gluten-free pizza crust, we bet you agree. There's no overlooking a lousy crust, even if it's delivering great toppings, sauce, and cheese.

In total, our home oven and kitchen cranked out more than 1,000 gluten-free pizzas in 2018. During our Year of Gluten-Free Pizza, every night was gluten-free pizza night, not just Sundays.

Peter with Giovanni Cesarano, pizzaiolo at New York's King Umberto and winner of the gluten-free division at the 2018 Caputo Cup.

The Time Has Come for World-Class Gluten-Free Pizza at Home

Overlooking the Mediterranean from Italy's Amalfi Coast

Pizza is a uniquely universal food and a surprisingly good chameleon. It can be simple or complex, common or gourmet. Pizzas are eaten for breakfast, lunch, dinner, and even dessert. They are enjoyed around the world by all different cultures with fantastically different cuisines.

Pizza unites people. Pretty much everyone eats—and loves—pizza (even if they do argue over toppings). Pizza is served everywhere, at family dinners, Super Bowl parties, school parties, and birthday parties, to name a few.

If you're gluten-free, you shouldn't have to miss out on that experience—and you shouldn't have to settle for a subpar pizza option. On the spectrum of gluten-free pizza, "Is a gluten-free pizza available?" shouldn't be the base metric by which you dole out praise. That's the lowest possible standard. Aspire for better. Demand better. Bake better. You deserve it.

Now, with this cookbook and these recipes, you can get what you deserve. **This isn't gluten-free pizza. This is pizza, gluten-free.** There's an importance difference between the two. And you're about to see and taste it.

Dal nostro tavolo senza glutine al tuo
(from our gluten-free table to yours),

PETER BRONSKI
Colorado, March 2019

Seven Secrets to Great Gluten-Free Pizza at Home

Here's the most-important secret you need to know about making great gluten-free pizza at home: It's not that hard. In fact, it's downright easy!

But if great gluten-free pizza is easy, why is there still so much lousy gluten-free pizza out there in the world? For one, some of the best gluten-free pizza is confined to a few pizzerias doing really exceptional things. And no one has figured out how to translate their secrets into the home kitchen and oven . . . until now.

You're holding in your hands the definitive manual for some of the best gluten-free pizza you've ever had. And best of all, you can make it with your own two hands in your kitchen at home. No pilgrimage to Italy required (though it is highly recommended!).

With that in mind, here are seven overarching secrets for ensuring success.

1. Time

Time is a crucial variable for gluten-free pizzas. You need enough of it to allow for the forty-eight-hour fermentations that can transform ordinary dough into a wondrous marvel. You need just the right amount of it for doughs that need to rise. You'll want to use as little of it as possible for pizzas that achieve their best selves when immediately fired. Using your time effectively means you can spend more time enjoying great gluten-free pizza and less time preparing it.

For example, many of our recipes eliminate the common par-baking of thin-crust pizzas, so that the fresh dough gets pressed out, topped, and fired in the oven just once, with fast bake times (less than ten minutes for thinner pizza styles). Incredibly, our Neapolitan pizza spends no more than five minutes in the oven!

2. Temperature

Like time, temperature is a crucial variable for any pizza. But you don't need a commercial-grade oven or an expensive, space-consuming, wood-fired pizza oven in your backyard preheated to 900°F (480°C) to bake an amazing gluten-free pizza. Leveraging your home oven and a few choice tools and techniques to expose your pizza dough to just the right amount of heat can be the difference between a flat, underwhelming crust and a puffy one with massive air pockets that would impress even experienced pizzaioli.

3. Tools

Don't expect to make mind-blowing gluten-free pizzas on the same light aluminum baking sheet you use for cookies. Aluminum baking sheets simply can't hold and transfer high oven heat to your pizza crusts like a baking steel. The inferior result is blond and floppy pizza crust, rather than the perfect balance of char and chew you can achieve with a baking steel. A modest investment (less than $150 total) in a few select pieces of equipment—a thick baking steel, a thin pizza peel—will do wonders for your at-home pizza making. And with prices for a basic, plain-cheese, gluten-free pizza hovering around $15 to $20-plus as of this writing, you'll pay off your investment in no time and start reaping the rich rewards of better gluten-free pizza than you can get at 95 percent of the pizzerias out there.

4. Ingredients

It feels cliché to say it, but quality ingredients make for quality pizza. But that doesn't have to mean *expensive* ingredients. You can grow a basil plant at home for pennies, and it'll supply a summer's worth of fresh basil to top your pizzas. Big-box retailers now carry canned San Marzano tomatoes for competitive, affordable prices. And when you're faced with paying a small premium for good ingredients, it's almost always worth it—and still cheaper than paying the expensive surcharge for subpar gluten-free pizza from the supermarket freezer section.

Don't overlook the importance of the gluten-free flours used for each pizza style in this book; they're optimized to the pizza style at hand. All-purpose gluten-free flour blends have become justifiability popular in baking as a 1:1 alternative to wheat flour, but no single all-purpose gluten-free flour blend can perform equally well for every pizza style. The specific flour combinations allow for each gluten-free pizza to reach its true potential.

5. Techniques

Gluten-free pizza can be great, but preparing it can also be . . . different. It often starts with wetter, stickier dough than its wheat-based counterpart. And making it at home versus in the controlled, high-temperature environment of commercial pizza ovens in pizzerias adds an additional challenge. Applying just the right techniques both a) makes your life a whole lot easier and b) unlocks gluten-free pizza possibilities you might not have thought possible.

6. Recipes

Recipes are what bring secrets 1 through 5 together. Without them, you have all the variables at your disposal but no good idea of what to do with them. It's like wanting to fly from New York to Naples and having fuel and the parts to build an airplane but no idea how to put it all together. Fortunately, if you're reading these words, you can put the recipes in this book to good use. We're biased, we know, but we're confident enough to say this book makes most other gluten-free pizza recipes obsolete, *including our own previously published ones*. If you are the (hopefully happy) owner of one of our previous gluten-free cookbooks, tear out those pizza recipes, recycle the pages, and use this book instead.

7. Practice

If our recipes are the *science* of gluten-free pizza making, your practice of making those pizzas is the *art*. There is finesse to great pizza making. The more you make pizza, the more practice you get. And the more practice you get, the easier the pizza making becomes. The pizzas themselves simply turn out better, too. This is true, even for professional pizzaioli. While in Naples, we visited Pizzeria Vesi twice. On each of the visits, different pizzaioli made our pizzas—and the pizza crusts were totally different. If we hadn't known better, we'd have guessed they were from two different pizzerias. The more comfortable you get with gluten-free pizza dough, the better your pizzas will get. So enjoy the ride. Don't be discouraged if your first pizzas don't turn out exactly like our photos. Stay the course. Glorious pizza pastures are ahead for you!

A few select pieces of equipment—for a total investment of less than $150—can transform your home kitchen and oven into a highly effective pizzeria.

Baking Steel

A baking steel is exactly what it sounds like: a heavy piece of steel placed directly on your oven rack for baking. Apart from our grilled pizzas and pan pizzas, all of our pizzas should be cooked directly on a preheated steel. In our experience, there is *nothing* like the way a heavy baking steel builds up heat and then transfers that heat to a pizza crust. Lightweight aluminum pizza pans and common baking stones are no substitute.

Look for a steel that is at least 14 inches (36 cm) long along its shortest side. This gives you enough surface to comfortably launch a 13-inch (33 cm) pizza. Baking steels typically come in two thicknesses: 1/8 inch (3 mm; weighing about 7.5 pounds/3.5 kg) and 1/4 inch (6 mm; weighing about 15 pounds/6.8 kg). We strongly recommend investing in the thicker, heavier steel. Its greater thermal mass will transfer heat to a pizza crust better and won't lose as much heat while doing so, minimizing the time it takes to come back up to temperature in between pizzas if you're making more than one.

> **TIP:** Start preheating your baking steel forty-five minutes to one hour before you plan to launch your first pizza. Even if your oven thermostat says that it has finished preheating, it will take longer for the steel to also come up to that temperature. If you're making a series of pizzas, allow five to ten minutes between each pizza so the baking steel can come back up to its preheated temperature.

P.S. Did you know that a 13-inch (33 cm) pizza has 69 percent more surface area than a 10-inch (25 cm) pizza and nearly 20 percent more than a 12-inch (30 cm) pizza, both common sizes for premade frozen gluten-free crusts?

Although lightweight aluminum pans just don't work, if you already own a baking stone and aren't ready to invest in a baking steel, you can still make pretty good pizza. With a stone, the bottom of the crust will be blonder, and some pizza styles, like our New York pies, will come out a little floppier. Compensate by adding an extra minute to the bake time. Other pizza styles, especially the Neapolitan, really require the steel. Our own baking stone has gone into permanent retirement since we developed these recipes.

Pizza Peel

A pizza peel is the paddle used to launch pizzas and remove them from the oven. Although wooden pizza peels are quite popular, we prefer a thin metal peel. Its sharper edge is easier to slip between the parchment paper and the pizza crust when stripping the parchment (more on that in "Techniques," page 22).

Pizza Cutter

Sure, you can use a good kitchen knife to slice your pizzas. But we prefer a proper pizza cutter. There are two popular options: a traditional pizza wheel or a rocking pizza cutter, which has a long, curved blade that you rock across the pizza to slice it in a single sweeping cut.

Parchment Paper

You won't find parchment paper in traditional pizza making, but it's one of our tricks of the gluten-free pizza trade. Because gluten-free pizza dough is wetter and stickier than traditional dough, you need a way to transfer it easily and efficiently from your work surface to the oven. Simply dusting a pizza peel with bench flour won't cut it, since the wet dough just sucks up that extra flour.

Parchment paper is our not-so-secret weapon, but it's only used to transfer the pizza into the oven. After two minutes or so, the parchment paper gets removed so the pizza can spend most of its bake time in direct contact with the preheated baking steel. Look for rolls of parchment at least 14 inches (36 cm) wide (similar to the minimum width of your baking steel), so that you can comfortably press out full-size 13-inch (33 cm) pizzas with at least a little room around the edges.

> **TIP:** Parchment paper comes in rolls, which gives the paper a natural bend when you cut it to size. Place the parchment on your work surface so that the bend goes down, not up. This will keep your sheet of parchment flat and smooth, and it won't curl up on you as you're trying to work with a dough.

Pizza Pans

Chicago, Sicilian, grandma, and Detroit-style pizzas are pan pizzas. If you're serious about making those pizza styles, it's worth investing in some combination of well-seasoned steel pans and/or *dark* heavy-duty aluminum pans with a durable nonstick finish. These types of pans ensure that your crust achieves the perfect crispness at the edges while still releasing easily from the pan.

Avoid using light-colored, raw/unfinished aluminum pans. Using them results in two undesirable outcomes: soggy pizza crust and "stuck" pizzas that only release from the pan with great difficulty. Save yourself the frustration and go straight to the recommended pan styles!

Digital Kitchen Scale

A quality digital scale is *indispensable* for any type of baking. If you don't already own one, making a modest investment in a quality digital kitchen scale will reap great rewards. Decent models are widely available for about $20. Common features to look for include the ability to toggle weight measurements between grams and ounces, accuracy down to one gram, max capacity of at least ten pounds (useful for mixing large batches of flour and dough, including the weight of the bowl), and a tare button to zero the scale.

Infrared Thermometer (optional)

This is entirely optional, but if you really want to take your gluten-free pizza making seriously, add an infrared thermometer to your arsenal. These thermometers are perfect for determining the temperature of a surface, without ever having to touch that surface. We use it to double check the temperature of our baking steel, which is especially useful when we're superheating the steel to make a Neapolitan pizza or checking that the steel has reheated to its original temperature after baking a pizza. Look for a model that can measure at least up to 700°F (370°C). *Note:* Some infrared thermometers top out around 600°F (315°C), not enough to measure the 625 to 650°F target (330 to 340°C) for our Neapolitan pizza recipe.

IMPORTANT: For gas ovens with an open flame, and recipes with the oven rack in its top position close to the top heating element, trim the parchment paper around the pizza. Leave about a one-inch (2.5 cm) border, so that large amounts of spare parchment aren't exposed and at risk of igniting. You'll still want to leave a small "tab" of longer paper to make the parchment easier to grab when removing it.

Ingredients

Flours

Pizza dough is little more than flour, water, salt, and yeast. Yet from these humble ingredients, an incredible variety of amazing pizza crusts are born. And precisely because the ingredients are so simple, the details matter: quality, technique, and the flour itself.

Not all wheat flour is the same—you might choose a bread flour or a cake flour depending on what you're baking, or perhaps an entirely different strain of wheat if you're making pasta. Pizza flours differ, too. Legendary Italian flour mills such as Caputo and Pizzuti offer different pizza flours geared for Neapolitan versus New York versus other pizza styles. And many pizzaioli take great pride in precisely *which* flour they use for their pizzas.

These lessons hold especially true for gluten-free pizza. It's tempting—for sake of convenience—to use a single all-purpose gluten-free flour blend for every pizza style you'd want to make. A number of well-known pizza flour mills and gluten-free brands now offer all-purpose gluten-free pizza blends to make any style of pizza under the sun. In fact, that has been our approach in previous cookbooks and on our website, with our signature Artisan Gluten-Free Flour Blend recipe, which we use across a wide range of gluten-free baking. Fuggedaboutit. Not in this cookbook.

In pursuit of our vision to deliver a true gluten-free pizza revolution, we threw the Artisan Gluten-Free Flour Blend into the proverbial garbage. In its place, we've created various gluten-free flour combinations tailored to each pizza style. The result is gluten-free pizza crusts unlike anything you've ever seen before!

TYPES OF GLUTEN-FREE FLOURS

The world of gluten-free flours and starches is wonderfully diverse. There are grain flours such as rice, corn, millet, quinoa, teff, and buckwheat; nut flours such as almond and coconut; bean flours such as garbanzo; root vegetable flours such as potato and tapioca; and so on.

If you were to make every pizza recipe in this cookbook, you'd use about a dozen gluten-free flours. That may sound like a lot, and we suppose it is. But that number includes specialty pizzas such as the Berliner, which calls for buckwheat flour, and the California crust, which calls for teff. In truth, about half a dozen flours will unlock 90 percent of this book's recipes for you. And you may have some of those flours in your pantry already for other gluten-free baking.

FLOUR GRIND: GO FOR GOLDILOCKS—NOT TOO COARSE, NOT TOO FINE

From one gluten-free flour to another, and from one brand to the next, you'll find a fairly wide variety in the fineness of the flour grind. Some are very fine (often labeled "superfine"). Others are coarse, with a rough feel almost like fine particles of sand when rubbed between your fingers.

We recommend using gluten-free flours with a medium (regular) fine grind, which we think of as the "Goldilocks" grind. Do NOT use superfine flours, which absorb moisture differently and change the texture of the finished pizza crusts, unless explicitly called for. Likewise, avoid gluten-free flours that are noticeably coarse, giving finished pizzas an undesirable gritty mouthfeel.

"TRULY" GLUTEN-FREE FLOURS: WATCH FOR CROSS-CONTAMINATION RISK

If you're following a gluten-free diet for medical reasons—such as celiac disease, nonceliac gluten sensitivity, or wheat allergy—it's important to avoid the risk of cross-contamination in the gluten-free flours you're using.

Some flours otherwise made from naturally gluten-free ingredients, such as buckwheat, are often processed in facilities and on machinery shared with gluten-containing

A NOTE ABOUT FLOUR SUBSTITUTIONS: We've carefully and extensively tested gluten-free flour combinations for each pizza dough style in this cookbook, tweaking ingredients and their proportions. The end result is, we dare say, revolutionary. But trust us when we say flour substitutions generally don't work. That may come as a disappointment, but it's the raw, honest truth. That said, do make substitutions as necessary to meet your dietary needs, such as swapping out potato starch if you're avoiding nightshades. We just can't attest to the outcome.

grains. In addition, some flour brands may have dual lines for their products, such as "normal" corn flour (which has a cross-contamination risk from processing) and a certified gluten-free corn flour.

We recommend using brands and flours that have obtained third-party gluten-free certification and/or where the manufacturer makes clear statements about dedicated gluten-free facilities and machinery as well as batch testing of gluten-free flours to ensure that any possible cross-contamination remains below the allowable twenty parts per million (ppm) limit for gluten-free foods. It's a precaution, but an important one when your health is on the table.

A NEW FLOUR ON THE BLOCK: DEGLUTINATED WHEAT STARCH(!)

In some parts of the pizza-making world, an ingredient known as deglutinated wheat starch (Italian: *amido di frumento deglutinato*) is finding favor among some well-known companies selling gluten-free pizza-flour blends and, by extension, the pizzerias making their gluten-free pizzas using those blends. It's already fairly prevalent in parts of Europe, and it is starting to show up more often in the United States as well.

Deglutinated wheat starch is basically a refined wheat starch (akin to cornstarch versus a more-complete corn flour) that has been specially processed to remove gluten to below the twenty ppm threshold. For a variety of reasons—including a personal preference for naturally gluten-free flours and a desire to keep our recipes fully wheat-free for sake of those allergic to wheat—**we do not use deglutinated wheat starch in any of our recipes**.

You don't need it to make great gluten-free pizza anyway. Of the twenty-plus pizzerias we visited in Italy during summer 2018, about half used the ingredient as a component of their gluten-free flour blend and half specifically avoided it. There was no correlation between its use and the best gluten-free pizzas. Truly world-class gluten-free pizzas are possible with 100 percent naturally gluten-free ingredients.

BENCH FLOUR

Bench flour is additional "working" flour not included in a dough recipe. It can be used to flour a work surface, a pizza peel, or even the dough itself, to prevent sticking. For traditional glutenous pizzas, wheat-based semolina is often the flour of choice.

Our favorite gluten-free bench flour is a blend of white rice flour and corn flour. We'll keep a half cup or so in a small bowl on the kitchen counter while we're making pizzas. You can also use white rice flour, brown rice flour, or another flour that's already called for in the dough recipe.

MEASURING FLOUR: BY WEIGHT, NOT VOLUME

There's only one way to confidently and accurately measure flours for pizza making: by weight, using a quality digital home kitchen scale. They're widely available and inexpensive (about $20). The result will be a better, more consistent pizza.

Alternatively, measuring by volume (i.e., by cup measure) simply doesn't measure up. In our own experiments, the weight of a cup of gluten-free flour can vary by as much as a whopping 44 percent depending on how loosely or tightly packed the cup is. That's just too much variability to get great gluten-free pizza, time after time. Measure your flours by weight down to the gram.

TRANSFORMING FLOUR INTO DOUGH

Mixing the right blend of gluten-free flours for each pizza style is only part of the equation. Transforming that flour into *dough* is a critical step, too.

Quick Doughs Versus Fermented Doughs

Setting aside important stylistic differences (e.g., New York, Neapolitan, Sicilian), there are two types of gluten-free pizza dough in this cookbook: quick doughs and fermented doughs. We sometimes offer both options for the same style of pizza.

Quick doughs are prepared fresh at the moment you want to make your pizza. They typically contain a little more yeast than their fermented counterparts. In some cases, they're *very* fresh: mixed together and then immediately shaped and fired in the oven. In other cases, they're prepared fresh, then shaped and left to rise for a specific period of time before baking.

Fermented doughs require some planning ahead on your part. They use a little less yeast than their quick counterparts and undergo a long, slow fermentation in the refrigerator for the forty-eight hours leading up to when you want to actually bake your pizzas. During that time, the flavor and structure of the dough both undergo a magical transformation. A forty-eight-hour ferment is the gluten-free sweet spot. We've tested shorter twenty-four-hour ferments, which are too brief to achieve the desired effect, as well as longer seventy-two-hour ferments, which yield no noticeable improvement.

Die-hard pizzaioli will often use a *biga*, *poolish*, or other method for preparing their doughs. These methods use a portion of dough fermented for at least forty-eight hours and mix it with a freshly prepared dough to create a single, unified ball of dough. We've tested those techniques as well but have opted for the *diretto* approach of using either 100 percent quick dough or 100 percent fermented dough.

Fermentation Versus Rise

Yeast works in two related but very different ways in our doughs: to *ferment* the dough and to *leaven* the dough.

The *fermentation* (Italian: *maturazione*) is the aforementioned long, slow, forty-eight-hour period during which the yeast develops the dough's flavor and structure. The *leavening* (Italian: *levitazione*) is the rise time certain doughs get before baking, during which they puff up with internal air pockets. Some pizzas use one technique primarily, while other pizzas use both.

Water

Like flour, water matters. In gluten-free pizza making, how *much* water you use to prepare your doughs will definitely push the boundaries of what you may be accustomed to with traditional pizzas.

HYDRATION

Pizza doughs are often defined by their hydration, which is simply the amount of water versus the amount of flour in a recipe, expressed as a percentage. For example, 100 grams of water in 100 grams of flour would be a dough with 100 percent hydration, while 75 grams of water in 100 grams of flour would have 75 percent hydration. One gram of water is equivalent to one milliliter.

In traditional pizza making, dough hydration typically ranges between 60 and 85 percent. One thing we've learned over and over again across more than a decade of gluten-free baking is that "wetter is better." In almost all cases, gluten-free doughs need to start wetter than their wheat-based counterparts in order to bake properly. In this cookbook, our gluten-free pizza dough hydrations range from 90 to more than 130 percent!

Because the doughs start wetter and stickier, this sometimes requires adapting different techniques and methods for handling and baking the dough, such as starting a New York thin-crust pizza on a piece of parchment paper until it's dry enough to bake directly on the cook surface. But don't worry; these techniques will soon become second nature, and you'll be baking amazing homemade gluten-free pizzas like you're a master pizzaiolo or pizzaiola!

RELATIVE GLUTEN-FREE HYDRATION

Hydration is the pizza-making equivalent of baker's percentages. In traditional pizza making, if you know the style of pizza you want to make and the typical range of hydration that dough would use, you can dial in a recipe for your particular oven and temperature. However, that general rule of thumb does *not* apply in gluten-free pizza making.

Gluten-free flours and starches absorb water at wildly different rates. That means that, depending on the component ingredients that make up your pizza flour blend, the same amount of water might yield one dough that's too wet to work with and another dough that's too dry to even consider shaping into a pizza. We call this idiosyncrasy *relative gluten-free hydration*.

Throughout this cookbook, we've optimized different gluten-free flour blends paired with a specific level of hydration to achieve the best possible pizza for a home oven. You never have to worry about relative gluten-free hydration. But if, by chance, you're tempted to adapt our recipes with—say—your favorite all-purpose gluten-free flour blend, be prepared to experiment with the overall hydration level until you've got it right.

Cheeses

MOZZARELLA

Let's be honest: In the world of pizza cheese, there's mozzarella . . . and there's everything else. Mozzarella's mild flavor, wonderful meltiness, and long-standing connection to pizza tradition make it the pizza-making cheese of choice.

As a result, for eight consecutive years, mozzarella has been the most-popular cheese in the country, overtaking even cheddar. Mozzarella accounts for nearly a third of per capita cheese consumption in the United States!

It's a wonderfully versatile—and naturally gluten-free—cheese that comes in a number of styles, many of which wc use throughout this cookbook. Here's what you need to know about each:

Buffalo Mozzarella Versus Fior di Latte

In Italy, standard mozzarella is buffalo mozzarella, made from the milk of the water buffalo. Unless otherwise specified, that's probably what you're getting on your Italian pizza. By contrast, *fior di latte* (literally "flower of the milk") is mozzarella made from cow's milk.

In the United States, the situation is exactly reversed. Unless otherwise specified or you're shopping at an Italian specialty foods importer, most forms of mozzarella sold in US supermarkets are cow's milk mozzarella.

Fresh Mozzarella

Pure, white, and high in moisture, fresh mozzarella is the classic choice for pizza styles such as Neapolitan. It typically comes packaged in one of two ways: 1) whole balls packed in water in 8-ounce (227-gram) containers or 2) in thermoform plastic packaging (either whole or presliced, without water).

We prefer fresh mozzarella packed in water, because it simply melts better. Fresh mozzarella packaged without water in shrink-wrapped plastic is too dry. As a pizza cheese, it acts like a hybrid of true fresh mozzarella and low-moisture brick mozzarella. If push comes to shove, either type will work in recipes that call for fresh mozzarella. Fresh mozzarella has a relatively short refrigerated shelf life, so buy it close to when you plan to use it.

The balls of fresh mozzarella come in a number of sizes. Three of the most common include *ciliegine* (little cherries, about 0.33 ounces/9 grams each), *bocconcini* (little bites, about 1.5 ounces/42 grams each), and *ovoline* (egg-size, about 4 ounces/115 grams each). Unless a recipe specifically calls for a certain size ball of fresh mozzarella, use whatever is available at your local market. Use your hands to tear larger ovoline into smaller pieces when topping a pizza.

Brick Mozzarella

Also known as low-moisture mozzarella, brick mozzarella cheese is drier and yellower than fresh mozzarella and is often sold in 16-ounce (454-gram) shrink-wrapped packaging. It can be sliced for pizza styles such as Sicilian or shredded on a box grater for pizza styles such as New York thin-crust.

These days you can often find a few types at markets with more extensive cheese selections, but you should typically be able to find whole-milk and part-skim varieties. Either will work in any recipes that call for brick mozzarella, though we prefer whole-milk varieties for their melting quality and flavor richness. Low-moisture mozzarella has a much longer refrigerated shelf life than fresh mozzarella, so stock up when it's on sale!

Pre-Shredded Mozzarella

Pre-shredded mozzarella is exactly what it sounds like. It's low-moisture brick mozzarella that's been shredded and packaged for your convenience.

But here's the catch: Pre-shredded mozzarella is tossed in an anticaking agent (such as potato starch or plant cellulose derived from wood pulp) to prevent the cheese strands from sticking together. As a result, it's even drier than low-moisture brick mozzarella, it doesn't melt nearly as well, and you'll need to make sure those anticaking agents are actually gluten-free.

We advise avoiding pre-shredded mozzarella. It takes just a minute (we've timed it!) to shred a one-pound brick of low-moisture mozzarella on a box grater, and the result is so much better. If you're going through the effort of making a homemade pizza, take this small extra step. It's worth it!

Burrata

Burrata is a close cousin of fresh mozzarella. It's a shell of fresh mozzarella filled with a blend of curd and cream. It generally has too much moisture to use as a pizza cheese pre-oven, but some recipes may call for it after cooking the pizza as a fresh finishing cheese.

Dairy-Free Mozzarella

A number of companies now offer varieties of vegan, plant-based, dairy-free mozzarella cheese. If you're following a gluten-free *and* dairy-free diet, these can be a good option, especially for any pizza styles that call for low-moisture brick mozzarella.

OTHER CHEESES

Mozzarella may be the cheese star of the pizza show, but throughout this cookbook, select recipes call for other cheeses such as provolone, Parmigiano-Reggiano, Pecorino Romano, and ricotta. Enough said!

Tomatoes

SAN MARZANO TOMATOES

The San Marzano tomato is to pizza sauce what mozzarella is to pizza cheese: the belle of the ball. It is an Italian variety of plum tomato prized for its sweet flavor and low acidity, which make it ideal for sauces.

The San Marzano designation can actually refer to three things: the strain of tomato, where the tomato is grown, and how the tomato is grown, harvested, and packed. Like any revered product, they're also prone to cheaper imitations. Here's what you need to know to navigate the canned-tomato section of your local market.

Italian Imported and Certified Tomatoes

"True" San Marzano tomatoes hail from the Sarnese-Nocerino region of Campania in southern Italy, where the tomatoes grow in the rich volcanic soils surrounding Mount Vesuvius. They must be peeled and canned whole or fileted (no diced or crushed allowed). Certified producers will have two seals that verify their authenticity: *Pomodoro San Marzano dell'Agro Sarnese-Nocerino* and *Denominazione d'Origine Protetta (DOP)*.

While some DOP-certified brands command premium import prices, we've also found DOP-certified San Marzano tomatoes sold for reasonable prices under the store brand label at our local American wholesale club.

There are also proper Italian brands that grow San Marzano tomatoes within the designated region but choose to forgo the costs of actually getting certified, as well as some Italian San Marzano–variety tomatoes grown outside the Sarnese-Nocerino region ineligible for DOP certification. Many are quite good.

American-Grown Tomatoes

American tomato companies aren't held to the same European Union labeling laws as Italian brands bearing the DOP seal and San Marzano name, so you have to be much more discerning.

Some American companies use the words *San Marzano* in their brand name. Canned tomato varieties claiming "San Marzano–style plum tomatoes" and "Italian-style tomatoes" are fairly ubiquitous in supermarkets, so it's easy to pay import prices for a domestic product. Even so, there are very good options that can stand up against the Italian originals.

Look for domestically grown San Marzano or similar plum tomatoes that have simple ingredient labels: peeled tomatoes, packed in tomato juice or tomato puree, with basil leaf. Some have a little added salt. We prefer brands that don't use preservatives or that use only citric acid (*not* calcium chloride).

American brands might sell diced or pureed "San Marzano" tomatoes. Avoid these. Buy only whole peeled tomatoes, because those cans contain the best-quality tomatoes. Then use a handheld immersion blender, food processor, or blender to puree the tomatoes to your desired consistency.

CAMPARI TOMATOES

For pizza styles that call for whole slices of fresh tomato, we love using heirloom varieties grown in our home garden. But when those aren't available, store-bought Campari tomatoes are our go-to variety.

Sometimes sold in American supermarkets as "tomatoes on the vine," Campari tomatoes are known as the "tomato lover's tomato." They're sweet, packed with flavor, a beautiful deep red color, ripened naturally (without ethylene gas), and available almost year-round (thanks to hydroponic growing techniques).

DATTERINI TOMATOES

From our grilled pizzas to the marinara sauce that tops our fried *montanara* pizza, when a recipe calls for halved and quartered grape or cherry tomatoes, the Italian *datterini* (meaning "little dates," for their shape and sweetness) are our favorite. Alas, they're seldom available in American supermarkets. Look for other sweet varieties of grape or cherry tomatoes, sometimes labeled as "salad tomatoes" or "snacking tomatoes." Don't worry too much about the particulars. As long as they're fresh and sweet, they'll work.

SUN-DRIED TOMATOES

Sun-dried tomatoes are typically sold in two ways: in glass jars packed in oil or dry in resealable bags. We strongly recommend the packed-in-oil varieties. Look for brands that use only pure extra virgin olive oil (some brands use a blend that can also include sunflower, safflower, or other oils). Likewise, some brands use sulfites to preserve color; we prefer sulfite-free brands that only preserve with salt.

Olive Oil

Olive oil plays three very different—but equally important—roles in our pizza recipes: 1) to improve the taste and texture of our gluten-free pizza doughs, 2) to makc heavily hydrated gluten-free doughs easier to handle, and 3) for flavor as a topping on finished pizzas. This calls for two different kinds of olive oil.

REFINED OLIVE OIL

Refined olive oil is the workhorse of many of our pizza recipes. It has a mild flavor and a higher smoke point suitable for high-temperature cooking. It goes by many possible names: refined olive oil, light olive oil, light tasting olive oil, extra light olive oil, extra light tasting olive oil. Regardless, *don't* confuse it with extra *virgin* olive oil.

Use refined olive oil whenever a recipe calls for olive oil before the pizza gets cooked, such as in the dough's wet ingredients, for coating the dough and/or your hands, or for brushing the surface of the pressed-out dough.

EXTRA VIRGIN OLIVE OIL

Extra virgin olive oil is essentially the fresh-pressed juice of olives. It has a lower smoke point than refined olive oil and a rich but delicate flavor. While you can certainly seek out an excellent imported Italian extra virgin olive oil, there are also great options from other countries throughout the Mediterranean region, not to mention excellent domestic extra virgin olive oils from states like California.

Use extra virgin olive oil as a finishing ingredient whenever a recipe calls for olive oil after the pizza is cooked, such as for drizzling on the pizza just before serving.

A few key techniques will go a long way toward making your gluten-free pizza preparation a lot easier. Don't worry, after practicing them a few times, they'll become second nature, and you'll be a master pizza maker in no time!

Pressing Out Dough with Oiled Hands

Pizza styles such as our New York, California, grilled, and buckwheat call for pressing out the dough on floured parchment using oiled hands:

- Generously coat the palms and fingers of your hands with olive oil.

- With your oiled hands, gently press the dough into a circle.

- Using the palm and heel of your hand (especially the fleshy part at the base of your thumb), work from the center outward to build up a small perimeter lip around the edge of the crust. If the recipe calls for no lip on the dough, simply press it flat.

- Add more olive oil to your hands as needed to prevent the dough from sticking.

On doughs with a lip, the pressed area of the dough should be thin, typically about 1/8 inch (3 mm) thick. The raised lip should be about 1/4 inch (6 mm) thicker and about 1/2 inch (13 mm) wide.

Pressing Out Dough with Floured Hands

Pizza styles such as our Neapolitan and *montanara* call for working the dough on floured parchment with floured hands:

- Coat the palms and fingers of your hands with superfine or regular rice flour. Sprinkle additional flour over the dough.

- Carefully tease out the dough into a wider circle using your fingertips. Sprinkle additional flour as needed to prevent the dough from sticking to your hands.

- As the dough gets wider and thinner, you can start using the heel of your hand to press the center area even flatter. But try to use your fingers to tease the edges wider still.

- Avoid forming creases and/or folds in the dough, especially in the *cornicione* area around the perimeter, which inhibit the cavernous air pockets that should form. (The cornicione is the untopped perimeter of dough that puffs into the crust on pizzas styles such as Neapolitan.)

For a Neapolitan-style pizza, the center should be very thin, almost see-through. Leave the slightest lip of raised dough around the perimeter, then flatten out that edge of dough. The raised, flattened lip should be about ⅛ inch (3 mm) thicker and about 1 inch (2.5 cm) wide.

Rolling Out Dough with a Rolling Pin

Ultrathin pizza styles such as our Roman cracker crust and the tavern pie call for working the dough on unfloured parchment with a rolling pin, using either flour or oil.

- Dust the surface of the dough and the rolling pin with bench flour (for Roman-style pizzas), or rub down the rolling pin with some olive oil (for tavern-style pizzas).

- Using the rolling pin, roll out the dough (many of our recipes call for an 11 x 14-inch [28 x 36 cm] rectangle).

- Roll the dough gently, working it a little at a time. This helps prevent excessive sticking to the rolling pin. If the rolling pin sticks to the dough, add a little more bench flour to the rolling pin and/or the sticky spot of dough. If using oil, rub additional oil onto the rolling pin.

- Once the dough is rolled to uniform thinness and appropriate shape and size, use a pizza wheel or sharp knife to trim away any jagged, uneven edges to leave a smooth, finished edge with slightly rounded corners. (Sharp corners will overcook and burn more easily.)

The rolled-out dough should generally be very thin, about ⅛ inch (3 mm) thick.

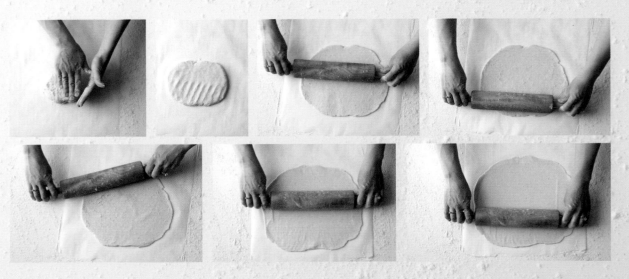

Stripping the Parchment

Shaping the dough on parchment paper and using that parchment to launch the pizza onto the baking steel is one of our key methods for working with wetter, stickier gluten-free doughs. But once the crust bakes enough (about two minutes), it's then time to "strip the parchment" and let the pizza finish its bake directly on the steel. That's where this technique comes in handy. You'll see it referenced repeatedly throughout this cookbook.

- Lightly dust the pizza peel with bench flour, especially along the leading edge of the peel.

- After the initial bake (usually about two minutes), carefully grab one corner of the parchment paper and rotate the pizza so the corner of the parchment is facing out of the oven.

- Coax the pizza peel under the leading edge of the pizza.

- In more or less one motion, gently pull on the parchment while slowly pushing the peel forward and lifting the pizza slightly, if necessary. The goal is to remove the parchment paper while leaving the pizza in place on the steel.

With a little practice, stripping the parchment out from under the pizza becomes an easy, quick, and simple motion. Do it as quickly as you safely can and immediately shut the oven door to retain as much heat as possible. Compost the parchment.

Superheating the Steel

Most home ovens can reach a maximum temperature of 550°F (285°C). With a preheated baking steel, that's plenty hot for many pizza styles. But select pizzas, including our Neapolitan recipes, benefit from a boost of added heat to achieve their full effect. Superheating your baking steel to 625°F (330°C) or greater makes a *world* of difference in the finished pizza. Following these steps can take the surface of your steel from 550°F (285°C) to 625°F (330°C) or more:

1. Place your oven rack in its top position and place the baking steel on it so that the steel is about 3 to 4 inches (7.5 to 10 cm) below the oven's broiler elements.

2. Set the oven to bake at 550°F (285°C) and preheat the steel for at least 45 minutes.

3. At the appointed time in a given recipe, switch the oven to its broil setting on high for at least 4 minutes.

The high-temperature broil should be *continuous*. If your oven's thermostat cycles the broiler element on and off during the four minutes—or if your oven overheats—leave the oven door ajar. This allows just enough hot air to escape for the broiler to remain on without the thermostat turning it off.

Switch your oven back to bake at 550°F (285°C) and launch your pizza as soon as possible while the steel is still superheated.

If you superheat the steel with the oven door ajar, close the door and then switch the oven back to bake at 550°F (285°C). Wait 1 to 2 minutes to allow the oven air temperature to climb back up before launching your pizza. But don't wait too long, because the steel will start to lose its superheated temperature.

Troubleshooting

With a little practice, you'll be making revolutionary gluten-free pizzas in no time. But if the pizzas don't turn out quite like you expect, or your experience doesn't match our photos and descriptions, start here with these basic troubleshooting tips. You can always also email us at info@nogluten-noproblem.com and we'll do our best to help, too.

Water

Our recipes should work with most any tap water, but differences in tap water can influence a dough's consistency. That said, no pizza dough should be tough to work or as thick as play dough. If your raw pizza dough turns out unexpectedly thick, check your tap water.

Hard water can result in tougher doughs. Most municipalities in the United States publish annual drinking water test results, where you can check the total hardness of your water. Kelli's parents in upstate New York have water that's on average *six times* harder than ours in Colorado.

If you happen to have very hard tap water and your home isn't fitted with a water softener, consider "thinning" the tap water with some distilled water. (*Don't* use mineral or spring waters, which can also be hard.)

Ovens

In theory, ovens are simple: Set the temperature and bake at that temperature. Right? Not always. Ovens can be variable, temperamental creatures. Some run hot, while others run cold. Some have hot and cold spots that will cook a pizza unevenly.

Use an oven thermometer to understand how accurate your oven's temperature is and compensate accordingly to cook at a recipe's specific temperature. If your oven has hot and cold spots, rotate the pizza halfway through baking to ensure even browning during the bake.

Electric and gas ovens can bake differently, too. Electric heating elements can give off residual heat even when they're off, and their zigzag pattern heats the baking steel fairly evenly across its surface area. By contrast, gas elements basically have "instant off" for their heat, and their broiler element might be a single flame tube down the center of the oven's ceiling, resulting in a hotter steel down the center line and cooler near the edges.

Learn your oven. Once you do, the two of you can dance together making wonderful gluten-free pizzas with the perfect balance of char and chew.

NOTE: If your oven has a "convection" bake setting, leave it off. We've designed these recipes for standard oven baking *without* a convection fan.

Flours

We've designed and tested this book's recipes to work with a wide range of brands and their flours. You shouldn't be held to a single brand to use their flours exclusively. But there *is* undoubtedly variability from one brand to the next in terms of the flavor strength of their flours and how finely they grind them. Don't be afraid to experiment with the same flours from different brands to achieve a better result.

Grills

Like ovens, grills vary widely: gas versus charcoal, the number of burners, potential hot spots, etc. Use our grilled pizza recipes as a guideline rather than a hard-and-fast set of rules you must follow. You may have to adjust temperature settings and/or grill time to achieve the desired results.

High-Altitude Adjustments

If you live at high altitude—5,000 feet (1,500 meters) or more above sea level—there are easy modifications you can make to our recipes. In fact, we think the high-altitude recipes are even *better* than the sea-level versions. (Of course, we live in Colorado, so we're also a bit biased.) The solution usually involves boosting the hydration of the dough while decreasing the leavening. Any high-altitude recipe modifications can be found in notes directly on the dough recipe pages.

Beyond Gluten-Free—Addressing Common Allergens and Dietary Considerations

Every recipe in this cookbook is delightfully wheat- and gluten-free. But it doesn't stop there. When it comes to the doughs that form the basis for each pizza, nearly every crust is Big-8 allergen–free, vegetarian, and vegan. That means no dairy, eggs, fish, shellfish, tree nuts, peanuts, or soy in the dough. There are just a handful of exceptions, and for some we provide substitution suggestions. Many of our pizza doughs are also corn-free and/or gum-free, and some are grain-free. As much as possible, the pizza doughs are what they call in Italy *pizza per tutti*—pizza for everyone!

	GLUTEN	WHEAT	CORN	DAIRY	EGGS	TREE NUTS	PEANUTS	SOY	XANTHAN GUM
New York–Style Pizzas									
Quick and Fermented Doughs									
Neapolitan Pizzas									
Neapolitan Dough									●
Thin-Crust Pizzas									
Roman Cracker Dough			●						●
Tavern Dough			●						●
Al Taglio Dough									●
Deep-Dish Pan Pizzas									
Chicago Deep-Dish Dough			●	◐					●
Traditional Chicago-style deep-dish pizza—including our gluten-free version—includes butter in the crust. However, you can easily make this recipe dairy-free and vegan by substituting a nondairy vegan shortening.									
Sicilian, Grandma, and Detroit doughs									

● **Indicates presence of an ingredient**

◐ **Indicates an option to modify the dough recipe to make it free of an ingredient**

* Note: This table focuses only on the pizza doughs and crusts. It does not include allergens for pizza toppings, so be sure to check the ingredients list for each recipe.

	GLUTEN	WHEAT	CORN	DAIRY	EGGS	TREE NUTS	PEANUTS	SOY	XANTHAN GUM
Grilled Pizzas									
Quick and Fermented Doughs						●			●

Our grilled pizza dough includes coconut flour. US Food and Drug Administration labeling laws require listing coconut as a tree nut, even though it is botanically considered a fruit. Most people with a tree nut allergy are still able to safely eat coconut. Please consult your primary care physician or allergist regarding whether coconut is safe to include in your diet

	GLUTEN	WHEAT	CORN	DAIRY	EGGS	TREE NUTS	PEANUTS	SOY	XANTHAN GUM
California-Style Pizzas									
Quick and Fermented Dough			●						●
Grain-Free Pizzas									
Farinata Dough									
Cauliflower Crust				●	●				
Zucchini Crust				●	●	◑			

Our zucchini crust uses almond flour. If you have a tree nut allergy, you can substitute another gluten-free flour, such as brown rice (although doing so would make the zucchini crust no longer grain-free as well).

	GLUTEN	WHEAT	CORN	DAIRY	EGGS	TREE NUTS	PEANUTS	SOY	XANTHAN GUM
Fried and Filled									
Montanara Dough									●
Calzone and Pizza Pocket Doughs									
Focaccia and Flatbread Pizzas									
Focaccia and Flatbread Doughs									
Buckwheat Pizza									
Buckwheat Dough			●						●
Backcountry Pizza									
Backcountry Dough									
Breakfast Pizzas									

Our breakfast pizzas are built on the New York–Style Dough and Roman Cracker Dough. See left.

Dessert Pizzas

Our dessert pizzas are all built on the New York–Style Dough. See left.

The Recipes

NEW YORK-STYLE PIZZAS

New York City is to American pizza what Naples is to Italian pizza: a historic epicenter. The region's rich Italian American heritage has given rise to a pizza culture with Italian roots and an American twist.

The classic New York–style thin-crust pizza is big and round, with a firm, chewy crust. It uses a sweet tomato sauce and shredded low-moisture mozzarella cheese. But above all else, it's defined by the pizza *slice*. A proper New York pizza allows you to hold and fold a slice in your hand, without that slice fracturing in half like a cracker or drooping like a soggy noodle.

Our gluten-free versions hit that coveted sweet spot. After all, as New York natives, we take our New York–style thin-crust seriously. All the pizzas in this section are based on two doughs: a quick version that can be prepared fresh and a fermented dough that requires a forty-eight-hour head start.

New York–Style Dough
Quick Version

⌐ MAKES ONE 12- TO 13-INCH (30 TO 33 CM) PIZZA ⌐

With a dough that's made fresh and doesn't require any rise time, this can be ready in a New York minute. The finished crust is soft and chewy, with just the right amount of char on the bottom to enable the slice fold and hold—the mark of any proper New York–style pizza.

200 grams warm water
(110°F/45°C)

1½ teaspoons sugar

1½ teaspoons active dry yeast

75 grams white rice flour

38 grams quinoa flour

38 grams tapioca starch

30 grams potato starch

11 grams potato flour

2 teaspoons ground
psyllium husk

¾ teaspoon salt

1 tablespoon olive oil

High-altitude modification: Increase the water to 213 grams and decrease the yeast to 1 teaspoon.

1. In a small bowl, whisk together the water, sugar, and yeast. Set aside to allow the yeast to activate, about 5 minutes, until foamy.

2. In a medium bowl, whisk together the rice flour, quinoa flour, tapioca starch, potato starch, potato flour, psyllium husk, and salt.

3. When the yeast mixture is foamy on top, add the oil and stir to combine.

4. Pour the yeast mixture into the flour mixture and stir vigorously with a spoon until it is smooth, there are no lumps, and it forms a thick dough.

Note: Although the New York quick dough doesn't require any rise time before topping and baking, we like pressing it out and giving it an optional 20- to 40-minute rise first.

New York–Style Dough

48-Hour Fermentation

∽ MAKES ONE 12- TO 13-INCH (30 TO 33 CM) PIZZA ∽

At a glance, this dough looks strikingly similar to our Quick Version. But something magical happens during the 48-hour fermentation. Both the flavor and the structure of the crust are superior to the quick dough. If you make this dough for your New York–style thin-crust pizzas, you won't regret it.

200 grams warm water
(110°F/45°C)

1½ teaspoons sugar

1 teaspoon active dry yeast

75 grams white rice flour

38 grams quinoa flour

38 grams tapioca starch

30 grams potato starch

11 grams potato flour

2 teaspoons ground
psyllium husk

¾ teaspoon salt

1 tablespoon olive oil, plus
more for greasing

High-altitude modification: Increase the water to 213 grams and decrease the yeast to ½ teaspoon.

1. In a small bowl, whisk together the water, sugar, and yeast. Set aside to allow the yeast to activate, about 5 minutes, until foamy.

2. In a medium bowl, whisk together the rice flour, quinoa flour, tapioca starch, potato starch, potato flour, psyllium husk, and salt.

3. When the yeast mixture is foamy on top, add the oil and stir to combine.

4. Pour the yeast mixture into the flour mixture and stir vigorously with a spoon until it is smooth, there are no lumps, and it forms a thick dough.

5. Lightly grease a medium-sized container (glass or plastic) with oil. Place the dough in the container and loosely cover. (If the container has a lid, place the lid on top of the container but do *not* snap it tightly shut. This allows excess carbon dioxide from the fermentation to escape while preventing the dough from drying out. Otherwise, covering the container with a plate or loosely with plastic wrap works well.)

6. Refrigerate for 48 hours.

7. At least 2 hours before you plan to make the pizza, remove the container from the refrigerator to allow the dough to come to room temperature.

Classic Cheese with Red Sauce

⤳ MAKES ONE 12- TO 13-INCH (30 TO 33 CM) PIZZA ⤳

A red-sauce cheese pizza is an Italian American classic. For this pizza, a great gluten-free crust is more important than ever, because there are no elaborate toppings or flavors to hide behind. This is New York–style pizza at its purest.

Bench flour (page 10)

1 prepared New York–Style Dough (pages 32 to 33)

Olive oil, for working the dough

½ cup (115 g) New York–Style Tomato Sauce (page 35)

6 ounces (170 g) shredded low-moisture mozzarella

1 teaspoon dried basil

1 teaspoon dried oregano

1. **If using the quick dough,** set your oven rack in the middle position, place your baking steel on it, and preheat the oven to 550°F (285°C) for 1 hour; do not start step 2 until the *end* of the preheat. **If using the fermented dough,** complete steps 2 to 4 *before* preheating the oven and let rise for 1 hour.

2. **To shape the dough,** place a 15-inch (38 cm) square piece of parchment paper on a flat surface. Sprinkle about 1 tablespoon bench flour onto the parchment.

3. Using a spatula, scrape the dough out of the bowl onto the center of the parchment.

4. With oiled hands, gently press the dough into a 12- to 13-inch (30 to 33 cm) circle, leaving a small lip of raised dough around the perimeter edge (see page 19 for technique tips).

5. **To finish the pizza,** ladle the sauce onto the crust and gently spread it in an even layer up to the raised edge.

Spread the mozzarella evenly over the sauce and then sprinkle the basil and oregano on top.

6. Use a lightly floured pizza peel to launch the pizza-on-parchment onto the baking steel in the oven. Bake for 2 minutes.

7. Strip the parchment (page 22). Bake for 6 to 7 more minutes with the pizza directly on the steel.

8. Remove the pizza from the oven and transfer to a large cutting board. Let set for 2 minutes, then slice and serve hot.

New York-Style Tomato Sauce

MAKES 3 CUPS (680 G)

The tomato sauce on New York–style pizzas is a little sweeter and more seasoned than the clean, simple San Marzano tomato sauce of Neapolitan pizzas. This no-cook sauce comes together in virtually no time. One batch is enough for several pizzas, so keep the extra sauce in your refrigerator for the next time you make pizza.

One 28-ounce (794 g) can whole peeled San Marzano tomatoes

One 6-ounce (170 g) can tomato paste

2 teaspoons dried basil

2 teaspoons dried oregano

2 teaspoons sugar

1 teaspoon garlic powder

1 teaspoon salt

Combine everything in a medium bowl. Use a handheld immersion blender, food processor, or blender to purée until almost smooth.

Rustic Pepperoni

◦ MAKES ONE 12- TO 13-INCH (30 TO 33 CM) PIZZA ◦

For years, pepperoni has retained the number one spot as America's favorite pizza topping. With a New York–style pizza, we prefer the large, sandwich-style cut with a blend of pepperoni and spicy Calabrese salami. A touch of freshly crumbled whole, dried oregano added after the pizza comes out of the oven results in a lovely finishing aroma.

6 thin slices (¾ ounce/ 20 g) sandwich pepperoni

6 thin slices (¾ ounce/ 20 g) Calabrese salami

Bench flour (page 10)

1 prepared New York–Style Dough (pages 32 to 33)

Olive oil, for working the dough

½ cup (115 g) New York–Style Tomato Sauce (page 35)

6 ounces (170 g) shredded low-moisture mozzarella

1 heaping tablespoon whole dried oregano

1. If using the quick dough, set your oven rack in the middle position, place your baking steel on it, and preheat the oven to 550°F (285°C) for 1 hour; do not start step 3 until the *end* of the preheat. **If using the fermented dough,** complete steps 3 to 5 *before* preheating the oven and let rise for 1 hour.

2. While the oven is preheating, heat a small sauté pan over low heat. Cook the pepperoni and salami on one side just until they begin to release some of their oil. Flip and repeat on the second side. Remove from the heat and set aside. (The goal is just to gently sweat the pepperoni and salami and not to fully cook them. They'll finish cooking in the oven on the pizza.)

3. To shape the dough, place a 15-inch (38 cm) square piece of parchment paper on a flat surface. Sprinkle about 1 tablespoon bench flour onto the parchment.

4. Using a spatula, scrape the dough out of the bowl onto the center of the parchment.

5. With oiled hands, gently press the dough into a 12- to 13-inch (30 to 33 cm) circle, leaving a small lip of raised dough around the perimeter edge (see page 19 for technique tips).

6. To finish the pizza, ladle the sauce onto the crust and gently spread it in an even layer up to the raised edge. Spread the mozzarella evenly over the sauce and distribute the pepperoni and salami on top.

7. Use a lightly floured pizza peel to launch the pizza-on-parchment onto the baking steel in the oven. Bake for 2 minutes.

8. Strip the parchment (page 22). Bake for 6 to 7 minutes with the pizza directly on the steel.

9. Remove the pizza from the oven and transfer to a large cutting board. Crush the oregano with your hands, sprinkling evenly over the pizza. Let set for 2 minutes, then slice and serve hot.

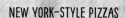

Sausage and Mushrooms

⌒∽ MAKES ONE 12- TO 13-INCH (30 TO 33 CM) PIZZA ∽⌒

Sweet Italian fennel sausage and sautéed mushrooms pack this pizza with umami flavors.

1 teaspoon olive oil, plus more for working the dough

4 ounces (115 g) sweet Italian fennel sausage (links or ground)

1 garlic clove, minced

4 ounces (115 g) button mushrooms, thinly sliced

Bench flour (page 10)

1 prepared New York–Style Dough (pages 32 to 33)

½ cup (115 g) New York–Style Tomato Sauce (page 35)

6 ounces (170 g) shredded low-moisture mozzarella

1. **If using the quick dough,** set your oven rack in the middle position, place your baking steel on it, and preheat the oven to 550°F (285°C) for 1 hour; do not start step 4 until the *end* of the preheat. **If using the fermented dough,** complete steps 4 to 6 *before* preheating the oven and let rise for 1 hour.

2. **While the oven is preheating,** heat the oil in small sauté pan over medium-high heat. Cut or break the sausage into small pieces. Brown until mostly cooked, about 5 minutes. Remove the sausage from the pan and set aside, leaving the oil in the pan.

3. Reduce the heat to medium and add the garlic, cooking until fragrant, about 30 seconds. Add the mushrooms and cook until all the water is released and evaporated, about 5 minutes, adding additional oil if the pan is too dry. Remove from the heat and set aside.

4. To shape the dough, place a 15-inch (38 cm) square piece of parchment paper on a flat surface. Sprinkle about 1 tablespoon bench flour onto the parchment.

5. Using a spatula, scrape the dough out of the bowl onto the center of the parchment.

6. With oiled hands, gently press the dough into a 12- to 13-inch (30 to 33 cm) circle, leaving a small lip of raised dough around the perimeter edge (see page 19 for technique tips).

7. To finish the pizza, ladle the sauce onto the crust and gently spread it in an even layer up to the raised edge. Spread the mozzarella evenly over the sauce and distribute the sausage and mushrooms on top.

8. Use a lightly floured pizza peel to launch the pizza-on-parchment onto the baking steel in the oven. Bake for 2 minutes.

9. Strip the parchment (page 22). Bake for 6 to 7 minutes with the pizza directly on the steel.

10. Remove the pizza from the oven and transfer to a large cutting board. Let set for 2 minutes, then slice and serve hot.

Hot Italian

Hot Italian sausage, peppers, and onions are this pizza's Holy Trinity.

1 teaspoon olive oil, plus more for working the dough

4 ounces (115 g) hot Italian sausage (links or ground)

1 small onion, thinly sliced

½ bell pepper, thinly sliced

Bench flour (page 10)

1 prepared New York–Style Dough (pages 32 to 33)

½ cup (115 g) New York–Style Tomato Sauce (page 35)

6 ounces (170 g) shredded low-moisture mozzarella

1. If using the quick dough, set your oven rack in the middle position, place your baking steel on it, and preheat the oven to 550°F (285°C) for 1 hour; do not start step 4 until the *end* of the preheat. **If using the fermented dough,** complete steps 4 to 6 *before* preheating the oven and let rise for 1 hour.

2. While the oven is preheating, heat the oil in a sauté pan over medium-high heat. Cut or break the sausage into small pieces. Brown until mostly cooked, about 5 minutes. Remove the sausage from the pan and set aside, leaving the oil in the pan.

3. Add the onion and pepper to the hot pan and sauté until the vegetables are soft and begin to caramelize, adding additional oil if the pan is too dry. Remove from the heat and set aside.

4. To shape the dough, place a 15-inch (38 cm) square piece of parchment paper on a flat surface. Sprinkle about 1 tablespoon bench flour onto the parchment.

5. Using a spatula, scrape the dough out of the bowl onto the center of the parchment.

6. With oiled hands, gently press the dough into a 12- to 13-inch (30 to 33 cm) circle, leaving a small lip of raised dough around the perimeter edge (see page 19 for technique tips).

7. To finish the pizza, ladle the sauce onto the crust and gently spread it in an even layer up to the raised edge. Spread the mozzarella evenly over the sauce and distribute the sausage, peppers, and onions on top.

8. Use a lightly floured pizza peel to launch the pizza-on-parchment onto the baking steel in the oven. Bake for 2 minutes.

9. Strip the parchment (page 22). Bake for 6 to 7 minutes with the pizza directly on the steel.

10. Remove the pizza from the oven and transfer to a large cutting board. Let set for 2 minutes, then slice and serve hot.

Tex-Mex Taco

Yes, Tex-Mex-inspired taco pizzas are a thing! This version uses the pizza crust as the base for taco meat and toppings.

8 ounces (225 g) ground beef

1⅛ teaspoons ground cumin

1 teaspoon chili powder

½ teaspoon salt

⅜ teaspoon ground black pepper

4 shakes hot sauce

⅓ cup (80 g) water

1 avocado

⅛ teaspoon garlic powder

3 teaspoons lime juice

2 Campari tomatoes (about 75 g), diced, with the liquid poured off

¼ small yellow onion (about 30 g), diced

1 garlic clove, minced

1 teaspoon minced jalapeño

Bench flour (page 10)

1 prepared New York–Style Dough (pages 32 to 33)

Olive oil, for working the dough

3 ounces (85 g) shredded low-moisture mozzarella

3 ounces (85 g) grated cheddar

½ cup (30 g) shredded lettuce

1 tablespoon chopped cilantro

1. If using the quick dough, set your oven rack in the middle position, place your baking steel on it, and preheat the oven to 550°F (285°C) for at least 1 hour; do not start step 5 until the *end* of the preheat. **If using the fermented dough,** complete steps 5 to 7 *before* preheating the oven and let rise for 1 hour.

2. While the oven is preheating, brown the beef in a large sauté pan over medium-high heat. Drain to remove all excess oil. Return the meat to the pan and add the chili powder, 1 teaspoon of the cumin, ¼ teaspoon of the salt, ⅛ teaspoon of the pepper, and the hot sauce. Cook for 1 minute. Add the water and cook until the water has evaporated. Remove from the heat and set aside.

3. In a small bowl, mash the avocado and season with the garlic powder, ⅛ teaspoon of the salt, ⅛ teaspoon of the pepper, and 1 teaspoon lime juice. Set aside.

4. In another small bowl, combine the tomatoes, onion, garlic, jalapeño, and the remaining 2 teaspoons lime juice, ⅛ teaspoon cumin, and ⅛ teaspoon each salt and pepper. Set aside.

5. To shape the crust, place a 15-inch (38 cm) square piece of parchment paper on a flat surface. Sprinkle about 1 tablespoon bench flour onto the parchment.

6. Using a spatula, scrape the dough out of the bowl onto the center of the parchment.

7. With oiled hands, gently press the dough into a 12- to 13-inch (30 to 33 cm) circle, leaving a small lip of raised dough around the perimeter edge (see page 19 for technique tips).

8. To finish the pizza, gently spread the beef in an even layer up to the raised edge. Spread the mozzarella and cheddar evenly over the meat.

9. Use a lightly floured pizza peel to launch the pizza-on-parchment onto the baking steel in the oven. Bake for 2 minutes.

10. Strip the parchment (page 22). Bake for 6 to 7 minutes with the pizza directly on the steel.

11. Remove the pizza from the oven and transfer to a large cutting board. Distribute the mashed avocado in small dollops over the pizza, then the tomato mixture, and then top with lettuce and cilantro. Let set for 2 minutes, then slice and serve hot.

Meat Lover's

Pork four ways—hot Italian sausage, smoky bacon, pepperoni, and ham—make this pizza a meat lover's dream.

1 teaspoon olive oil, plus more for working the dough

3 ounces (85 g) hot Italian sausage (links or ground)

4 slices bacon, diced

Bench flour (page 10)

1 prepared New York–Style Dough (pages 32 to 33)

½ cup (115 g) New York–Style Tomato Sauce (page 35)

6 ounces (170 g) shredded low-moisture mozzarella

2 ounces (55 g) small "coin" pepperoni

2 thick slices (3 ounces/85 g) cooked ham, diced into ¼-inch (6 mm) pieces

1 heaping tablespoon whole dried oregano

1. **If using the quick dough,** set your oven rack in the middle position, place your baking steel on it, and preheat the oven to 550°F (285°C) for 1 hour; do not start step 4 until the *end* of the preheat. **If using the fermented dough,** complete steps 4 to 6 *before* preheating the oven and let rise for 1 hour.

2. **While the oven is preheating,** heat the oil in a small sauté pan over medium-high heat. Cut or break the sausage into small pieces. Brown until mostly cooked, about 5 minutes. Remove the sausage and set aside, leaving the oil in the pan.

3. Add the bacon to the pan, cooking until just crispy. Drain the bacon on a paper towel and allow to cool.

4. **To shape the dough,** place a 15-inch (38 cm) square piece of parchment paper on a flat surface. Sprinkle about 1 tablespoon bench flour onto the parchment.

5. Using a spatula, scrape the dough out of the bowl onto the center of the parchment.

6. With oiled hands, gently press the dough into a 12- to 13-inch (30 to 33 cm) circle, leaving a small lip of raised dough around the perimeter edge (see page 19 for technique tips).

7. **To finish the pizza,** ladle the sauce onto the crust and gently spread it in an even layer up to the raised edge. Spread the mozzarella evenly over the sauce and distribute the pepperoni, ham, sausage, and bacon on top.

8. Use a lightly floured pizza peel to launch the pizza-on-parchment onto the baking steel in the oven. Bake for 2 minutes.

9. Strip the parchment (page 22). Bake for 6 to 7 minutes with the pizza directly on the steel.

10. Remove the pizza from the oven and transfer to a large cutting board. Crush the oregano with your hands and sprinkle over the pizza. Let set for 2 minutes, then slice and serve hot.

Buffalo Chicken

⌘ MAKES ONE 12- TO 13-INCH (30 TO 33 CM) PIZZA ⌘

The spicy flavor of Buffalo wing sauce on this chicken pizza makes
it perfect for watching your favorite sporting event.

3 tablespoons (45 g)
butter

1½ tablespoons white
rice flour

½ cup (120 ml) milk

⅓ cup (80 ml) hot sauce,
such as Frank's RedHot
Original

1 cup (115 g) Shredded
Chicken (page 173)

Bench flour (page 10)

1 prepared New York–Style
Dough (pages 32 to 33)

Olive oil, for working
the dough

6 ounces (170 g) shredded
low-moisture mozzarella

2 green onions, green part
only, chopped

Blue Cheese Dressing
(page 47), optional

1. If using the quick dough, set your oven rack in the middle position, place your baking steel on it, and preheat the oven to 550°F (285°C) for at least 1 hour; do not start step 4 until the *end* of the preheat. **If using the fermented dough,** complete steps 4 to 6 *before* preheating the oven and let rise for 1 hour.

2. While the oven is preheating, melt the butter in a small saucepan over medium-high heat. Stir in the rice flour and cook for 1 minute. Add the milk, whisking until the mixture thickens. Add the hot sauce and whisk until smooth. Remove from the heat.

3. Toss the chicken in ¼ cup (60 ml) of the prepared sauce and set aside. Reserve the remaining sauce.

4. To shape the dough, place a 15-inch (38 cm) square piece of parchment paper on a flat surface. Sprinkle about 1 tablespoon bench flour onto the parchment.

5. Using a spatula, scrape the dough out of the bowl onto the center of the parchment.

6. With oiled hands, gently press the dough into a 12- to 13-inch (30 to 33 cm) circle, leaving a small lip of raised dough around the perimeter edge (see page 19 for technique tips).

7. To finish the pizza, spread the remaining sauce gently onto the crust in an even layer up to the raised edge. Sprinkle the mozzarella evenly over the sauce and distribute the chicken on top.

8. Use a lightly floured pizza peel to launch the pizza-on-parchment onto the baking steel in the oven. Bake for 2 minutes.

9. Strip the parchment (page 22). Bake for 6 to 7 minutes with the pizza directly on the steel.

10. Remove the pizza from the oven and transfer to a large cutting board. Top with green onion and drizzle with the Blue Cheese Dressing or serve on the side, if desired. Let set for 2 minutes, then slice and serve hot.

Blue Cheese Dressing

MAKES 2/3 CUP (150 ML)

- **2 ounces (55 g) blue cheese (double-check gluten-free status)**
- **⅓ cup (80 g) sour cream**
- **2 tablespoons mayonnaise**
- **2 teaspoons apple cider vinegar**
- **2 teaspoons lemon juice**
- **¼ teaspoon sugar**
- **⅛ teaspoon garlic powder**
- **⅛ teaspoon salt**
- **⅛ teaspoon ground black pepper**
- **1 tablespoon milk, plus more for thinning**

Combine all ingredients in a blender and blend until smooth. Add more milk for a thinner dressing. Store in an airtight container in the refrigerator for up to 1 week.

Hawaiian

⤳ MAKES ONE 12- TO 13-INCH (30 TO 33 CM) PIZZA ⤳

Pineapple and ham are the costars of this pizza. We gently precook the pineapple to drive out extra moisture so it doesn't turn your pizza into a wet, soggy mess. For the red sauce, we use puréed San Marzano tomatoes versus our sweeter New York–style red sauce, to balance out the sweetness of the pineapple.

2 ounces (55 g) fresh pineapple or canned pineapple rings, diced

Bench flour (page 10)

1 prepared New York–Style Dough (pages 32 to 33)

Olive oil, for working the dough

½ cup (115 g) puréed canned San Marzano tomatoes

6 ounces (170 g) shredded low-moisture mozzarella

3 ounces (85 g) diced cooked ham or Canadian bacon

1. If using the quick dough, set your oven rack in the middle position, place your baking steel on it, and preheat the oven to 550°F (285°C) for 1 hour; do not start step 3 until the *end* of the preheat. **If using the fermented dough,** complete steps 3 to 5 *before* preheating the oven and let rise for 1 hour.

2. While the oven is preheating, heat a small sauté pan over medium-high heat. Add the pineapple and cook until all surface moisture has evaporated, about 4 minutes. Set aside.

3. To shape the dough, place a 15-inch (38 cm) square piece of parchment paper on a flat surface. Sprinkle about 1 tablespoon bench flour onto the parchment.

4. Using a spatula, scrape the dough out of the bowl onto the center of the parchment.

5. With oiled hands, gently press the dough into a 12- to 13-inch (30 to 33 cm) circle, leaving a small lip of raised dough around the perimeter edge (see page 19 for technique tips).

6. To finish the pizza, ladle the tomatoes onto the crust and gently spread in an even layer up to the raised edge. Spread the mozzarella evenly over the tomatoes and distribute the ham and pineapple on top.

7. Use a lightly floured pizza peel to launch the pizza-on-parchment onto the baking steel in the oven. Bake for 2 minutes.

8. Strip the parchment (page 22). Bake for 6 to 7 minutes with the pizza directly on the steel.

9. Remove the pizza from the oven and transfer to a large cutting board. Let set for 2 minutes, then slice and serve hot.

Premade Frozen Crust

∽ MAKES ONE 11-INCH (28 CM) PIZZA ∽

If you're looking for the convenience of having premade pizza crusts ready to go in your freezer, this recipe will beat any store-bought version. Make a few ahead of time and have them ready to go when the pizza craving strikes!

Bench flour
  (page 10)

1 prepared New
  York–Style Dough
  (Quick Version,
  page 32)

Olive oil, for working
  the dough

Note: This recipe uses the same amount of dough as our 12- to 13-inch (30 to 33 cm) New York pizzas but has an 11-inch (28 cm) diameter. This a) keeps the crust just a little thicker to help it stand up to the heat of the par-bake without the benefit of sauce, cheese, and toppings and b) allows the crust to easily fit into extra-large ziplock plastic storage bags. (Ziplock bags are now accepted at stores that have a plastic bag recycling program.)

1. Set your oven rack in the middle position and place your baking steel on it. Preheat the oven to 550°F (285°C) for 1 hour.

2. To shape the dough, place a 15-inch (38 cm) square piece of parchment paper on a flat surface. Sprinkle about 1 tablespoon bench flour onto the parchment.

3. Using a spatula, scrape the dough out of the bowl onto the center of the parchment.

4. With oiled hands, gently press the dough into a 11-inch (28 cm) circle, leaving a small lip of raised dough around the perimeter edge (see page 11 for technique tips).

5. To par-bake the crust, use a lightly floured pizza peel to launch the crust-on-parchment onto the baking steel in the oven. Bake for 2 minutes.

6. Strip the parchment (page 22). Bake for 6 to 7 minutes with the crust directly on the steel.

7. Remove the crust from the oven and transfer to a wire rack. Let cool.

8. Place the cooled crust in an extra-large ziplock bag (12 inches/30 cm square or larger) and place flat in the freezer. (Set the crust on a baking sheet in the freezer to keep it flat until it's fully frozen.) Multiple crusts, separated by parchment paper, can be stored in one bag if it is large enough.

9. To finish a pizza on the frozen crust, set your oven rack in the middle position and preheat the oven to 475°F (245°C).

10. When the oven is preheated, remove the crust from the freezer. Place on a baking sheet. Add sauce, cheese, and desired toppings to your pizza.

11. Bake for 9 minutes.

12. Remove the pizza from the oven and transfer to a large cutting board. Let set for 2 minutes, then slice and serve hot.

NEAPOLITAN
PIZZAS

The Neapolitan pizzas from their namesake Naples, Italy, are legendary. Authentic Neapolitan pizzas cook in just ninety seconds in insanely hot ovens that reach 900°F (480°C) or more. That blistering heat puffs the *cornicione*—the rim of crust around the perimeter of the pizza—to seriously impressive, airy heights.

Per both tradition and the Associazione Verace Pizza Napoletana (the governing body that defines a "true" Neapolitan pizza), these pizzas use San Marzano tomatoes, fresh mozzarella, and fresh basil. Additional toppings are, of course, optional.

This pizza style is one of the hardest to replicate in home ovens, largely because it's impossible to achieve the kind of temperatures you find in Neapolitan pizza ovens in a home kitchen. The challenge is even greater for gluten-free pizzas.

This section's pizzas are all based on a single dough. From start to finish, the pizza spends a grand total of just five minutes in the oven. And the gluten-free cornicione impressively puffs with cavernous air pockets. Seeing—and eating—is believing.

Neapolitan Dough

⤳ MAKES ONE 11-INCH (28 CM) PIZZA ⤲

The cornicione of Neapolitan pizzas are like fingerprints: No two are exactly alike. Each pizza crust puffs and blisters a bit differently in the heat. So, too, with our gluten-free version.

100 grams warm water
  (110°F/45°C)

1 teaspoon sugar

1 teaspoon active dry yeast

20 grams millet flour

20 grams potato starch

20 grams quinoa flour

20 grams tapioca starch

10 grams brown rice flour

½ teaspoon ground
  psyllium husk

½ teaspoon salt

½ teaspoon xanthan gum

2 tablespoons olive oil

*High-altitude modification:
Increase the water to
113 grams.*

1. In a small bowl, whisk together the water, sugar, and yeast. Set aside to allow the yeast to activate, about 5 minutes, until foamy.

2. In a medium bowl, whisk together the millet flour, potato starch, quinoa flour, tapioca starch, rice flour, psyllium husk, salt, and xanthan gum.

3. When the yeast mixture is foamy on top, add the oil and stir to combine.

4. Pour the yeast mixture into the flour mixture and stir vigorously with a spoon until it is smooth, there are no lumps, and it forms a loose dough.

Note: This is one of our most-hydrated pizza doughs, but with a little practice, you'll be cranking out consistently impressive gluten-free pizze *Napoletana* in no time. The fresher this dough, the better it performs. Be sure to preheat the oven before making the dough, then immediately shape, top, and fire it for the best results. We prefer using superfine rice flour to press out the dough. This is the only time in this book we call for superfine flour. If you don't have superfine rice flour and don't want to buy some just for this purpose, go ahead and use the same regular brown rice flour used in the dough recipe.

Neapolitan Margherita

∽ MAKES ONE 11-INCH (28 CM) PIZZA ∾

This is the classic Neapolitan pizza: San Marzano tomatoes and fresh mozzarella, finished with fresh basil leaf and a light drizzle of extra virgin olive oil. During our gluten-free pizza travels throughout Italy, we ordered at least one of these at every Neapolitan pizzeria we visited, from Pizzeria Vesi on Naples's famous Via Tribunali to Acqu'e Sale in Sorrento, with its sweeping view of Mount Vesuvius across the Bay of Naples.

1 recipe Neapolitan Dough (page 55; prepared after preheating the oven)

Bench flour (page 10)

Superfine rice flour, for working the dough

¼ cup (55 g) puréed canned San Marzano tomatoes

3 ounces (85 g) fresh mozzarella

1 tablespoon light olive oil

Coarse kosher salt

Extra virgin olive oil

5 basil leaves

1. Set your oven rack in the top position (3 to 4 inches [7.5 to 10 cm] below the oven's broiler elements) and place your baking steel on it. Preheat the oven to 550°F (285°C) for at least 45 minutes.

2. After preheating, make the Neapolitan Dough (page 55).

3. Immediately before shaping the dough, superheat the baking steel (page 22).

4. To shape the dough, place a 15-inch (38 cm) square piece of parchment paper on a flat surface. Sprinkle about 2 teaspoons bench flour onto the parchment.

5. Using a spatula, scrape the dough out of the bowl onto the center of the parchment and smooth the dough.

6. Coat your fingers and hands with superfine rice flour and sprinkle additional flour over the dough. Carefully tease the dough into an 11-inch (28 cm) circle, sprinkling just enough additional flour to prevent the dough from sticking to your hands (see page 20 for technique tips). The center area should be very thin;

leave about a 1-inch (2.5 cm) border for the slightly thicker cornicione (about 1/8 inch/3 mm thick).

7. To finish the pizza, set the oven from broil back to bake at 550°F (285°C). (If you had the oven door ajar to keep the broiler firing, close the oven door now to trap heat.)

8. Ladle the tomatoes onto the crust and gently spread in an even layer up to the cornicione. Tear the mozzarella into pieces and distribute evenly over the sauce. Brush the cornicione with the light olive oil until the dough glistens but does not have any standing pools of oil.

9. Remove any extra flour from around the edge of the pizza. Then use a lightly floured pizza peel to launch the pizza-on-parchment onto the baking steel in the oven. Bake for 2 minutes.

10. Strip the parchment (page 22). Bake for 2 to 3 minutes with the pizza directly on the steel, until the cornicione is golden brown.

11. Remove the pizza from the oven and transfer to a large cutting board. Sprinkle with the salt and drizzle with extra virgin olive oil. Place the basil leaves on top. Let set for 2 minutes, then slice and serve hot.

Wild Mushroom

⌒ MAKES ONE 11-INCH (28 CM) PIZZA ⌒

Did you know that mushrooms are the number two most popular pizza topping, behind only pepperoni? This white pizza's medley of mushrooms delivers in spades.

2 tablespoons light olive oil

1 garlic clove, minced

3 ounces (85 g) assorted mushrooms (e.g., cremini, oyster, chanterelle, shiitake), chopped

⅛ teaspoon salt

⅛ teaspoon ground black pepper

1 recipe Neapolitan Dough (page 55; prepared *after* preheating the oven)

Bench flour (page 10)

Superfine rice flour, for working the dough

3 ounces (85 g) fresh mozzarella

Extra virgin olive oil

5 basil leaves

1. Set your oven rack in the top position (3 to 4 inches [7.5 to 10 cm] below the oven's broiler elements) and place your baking steel on it. Preheat the oven to 550°F (285°C) for at least 45 minutes.

2. While the oven is preheating, heat 1 tablespoon of the light olive oil in a small sauté pan over medium-high heat. Add the garlic and cook until fragrant, about 30 seconds. Add the mushrooms, salt, and pepper and cook until all of the water is released and evaporated, about 5 minutes. Remove from the heat and set aside.

3. After preheating, make the Neapolitan Dough (page 55).

4. Immediately before shaping the dough, superheat the baking steel (page 22).

5. To shape the dough, place a 15-inch (38 cm) square piece of parchment paper on a flat surface. Sprinkle about 2 teaspoons bench flour onto the parchment.

6. Using a spatula, scrape the dough out of the bowl onto the center of the parchment and smooth the surface of the dough.

7. Coat your fingers and hands with superfine rice flour and sprinkle additional flour over the dough. Carefully tease the dough into an 11-inch (28 cm) circle, sprinkling just enough additional flour to prevent the dough from sticking to your hands (see page 20 for technique tips). The center area should be very thin;

leave about a 1-inch (2.5 cm) border for the slightly thicker cornicione (about ⅛ inch/ 3 mm thick).

8. To finish the pizza, set the oven from broil back to bake at 550°F (285°C). (If you had the oven door ajar to keep the broiler firing, close the oven door now to trap heat.)

9. Tear the mozzarella and distribute evenly over the dough, then distribute the mushrooms across the top of the pizza. Brush the cornicione with the remaining light olive oil, until the dough glistens but does not have any standing pools of oil.

10. Remove any extra flour from around the edge of the pizza. Then use a lightly floured pizza peel to launch the pizza-on-parchment onto the baking steel in the oven. Bake for 2 minutes.

11. Strip the parchment (page 22). Bake for 2 to 3 minutes with the pizza directly on the steel, until the cornicione is golden brown.

12. Remove the pizza from the oven and transfer to a large cutting board. Drizzle lightly with extra virgin olive oil. Place the basil leaves on top. Let set for 2 minutes, then slice and serve hot.

Ligurian Pesto

⦿ MAKES ONE 11-INCH (28 CM) PIZZA ⦿

In the small town of Marzana on the northern outskirts of Verona, Italy, you'll find Pizzeria Focacceria Quattrocento. Pizzaiolo Federico De Silvestri is a back-to-back winner in the gluten-free division of the prestigious World Pizza Championship. He and his wife, Mara, moved to Marzana with their children from the Ligurian coast, the source of inspiration for one of the best pesto pizzas we've ever had. Let this Neapolitan version transport you to Italy's Ligurian coastline.

1 recipe Neapolitan dough (page 55; prepared *after* preheating the oven)

Bench flour (page 10)

Superfine rice flour (for working the dough)

3 ounces (85 g) fresh mozzarella

2 ounces (55 g) grape tomatoes, sliced in half

1 tablespoon light olive oil

Coarse kosher salt

Extra virgin olive oil

2 tablespoons Pesto (page 61)

1. Set your oven rack in the top position (3 to 4 inches [7.5 to 10 cm] below the oven's broiler elements) and place your baking steel on it. Preheat the oven to 550°F (285°C) for at least 45 minutes.

2. After preheating, make the Neapolitan Dough (page 55).

3. Immediately before shaping the dough, superheat the baking steel (page 22).

4. To shape the dough, place a 15-inch (38 cm) square piece of parchment paper on a flat surface. Sprinkle about 2 teaspoons bench flour onto the parchment.

5. Using a spatula, scrape the dough out of the bowl onto the center of the parchment and smooth the surface of the dough.

6. Coat your fingers and hands with superfine rice flour and sprinkle additional flour over the dough. Carefully tease the dough into an 11-inch (28 cm) circle, sprinkling just enough additional flour to prevent the dough from sticking to your hands (see page 000 for technique tips). The center area should be very thin; leave about a 1-inch (2.5 cm) border for the slightly thicker cornicione (about ⅛ inch/ 3 mm thick).

7. To finish the pizza, set the oven from broil back to bake at 550°F (285°C). (If you had the oven door ajar to keep the broiler firing, close the oven door now to trap heat.)

8. Tear the mozzarella into pieces and distribute evenly over the dough, then scatter the halved grape tomatoes on top. Brush the exposed cornicione with the light olive oil, until the dough glistens but does not have any standing pools of oil.

9. Remove any extra flour from around the edge of the pizza. Then use a lightly floured pizza peel to launch the pizza-on-parchment onto the baking steel in the oven. Bake for 2 minutes.

10. Strip the parchment (page 22). Bake for 2 to 3 minutes with the pizza directly on the steel, until the cornicione is golden brown.

11. Remove the pizza from the oven and transfer to a large cutting board. Sprinkle with the salt and drizzle lightly with extra virgin olive oil. Drizzle the Pesto on top. Let set for 2 minutes, then slice and serve hot.

Pesto

MAKES 1 CUP (240 G)

2 cups (35 g) loosely packed basil leaves

1 garlic clove

2 tablespoons pine nuts

2 tablespoons grated Parmesan

Pinch salt

Pinch ground black pepper

½ cup (120 ml) extra virgin olive oil

Combine the basil, garlic, pine nuts, Parmesan, salt, and pepper in a food processor or blender and pulse to combine. Drizzle the oil in slowly and continue to blend until the mixture forms a smooth sauce. Refrigerate any unused pesto in an airtight container for up to 1 week.

Diavola

You know a pizzeria must be good when a pizzaiolo from another pizzeria recommends it. That's how we ended up at Kesté in the Financial District of lower Manhattan. There, pizzaiolo Roberto Caporuscio and his pizzaiola daughter, Giorgia, have brought Neapolitan pizza to the heart of New York City, with some of the best gluten-free pizza we've had, including a spicy *diavola*.

2 tablespoons olive oil

1 garlic clove, minced

¼ teaspoon red pepper flakes

Bench flour (page 10)

1 recipe Neapolitan Dough (page 55; prepared *after* preheating the oven)

Superfine rice flour, for working the dough

¼ cup (55 g) puréed canned San Marzano tomatoes

3 ounces (85 g) fresh mozzarella

6 thin slices (¾ ounce/20 g) sandwich pepperoni

5 basil leaves

1. Set your oven rack in the top position (3 to 4 inches [7.5 to 10 cm] below the oven's broiler elements) and place your baking steel on it. Preheat the oven to 550°F (285°C) for at least 45 minutes.

2. While the oven is preheating, mix 1 tablespoon of the oil with the garlic and red pepper flakes in a small bowl and set aside.

3. After preheating, make the Neapolitan Dough (page 55).

4. Immediately before shaping the dough, superheat the baking steel (page 22).

5. To shape the dough, place a 15-inch (38 cm) square piece of parchment paper on a flat surface. Dust about 2 teaspoons bench flour onto the parchment.

6. Using a spatula, scrape the dough out of the bowl onto the center of the parchment and smooth the dough.

7. Coat your fingers and hands with superfine rice flour and sprinkle additional flour over the dough. Carefully tease the dough into an 11-inch (28 cm) circle, sprinkling just enough additional flour to prevent the dough from sticking to your hands (see page 20 for technique tips). The center area should be very thin; leave about a 1-inch (2.5 cm) border for the slightly thicker cornicione (about ⅛ inch/3 mm thick).

8. To finish the pizza, set the oven from broil back to bake at 550°F (285°C). (If you had the oven door ajar to keep the broiler firing, close the oven door now to trap heat.)

9. Ladle the tomatoes onto the crust and gently spread in an even layer up to the cornicione. Tear the mozzarella into pieces and distribute evenly over the sauce. Scatter the pepperoni over the pizza, then spoon the spicy garlic oil on top. Brush the cornicione with the remaining tablespoon of oil, until the dough glistens but does not have any standing pools of oil.

10. Remove any extra flour from around the edge of the pizza. Then use a lightly floured pizza peel to launch the pizza-on-parchment onto the baking steel in the oven. Bake for 2 minutes.

11. Strip the parchment (page 22). Bake for 2 to 3 minutes with the pizza directly on the steel, until the cornicione is golden brown.

12. Remove the pizza from the oven and transfer to a large cutting board. Place the basil leaves on top. Let set for 2 minutes, then slice and serve hot.

THIN-CRUST PIZZAS

Gluten-free pizzas—especially those prepared on premade frozen crusts—are often criticized for being too thin, hard, and bland, like a cracker. But there's absolutely a time and place for thin, ultrathin, and even cracker-like pizza crusts. In fact, a number of regional pizza styles are defined by those crusts: the Roman cracker crust, the New Jersey bar pie, the Chicago tavern pie, the St. Louis–style pizza, and our version of the Roman al taglio pizza, to name a few.

Unlike the dense, flavorless gluten-free cracker crusts you've probably experienced, the recipes in this chapter are based on a pair of doughs that redefine the standard: crusts with real flavor, that are light and easy to eat, and that blister with myriad air pockets despite being ultrathin. It's time to give gluten-free thin-crust pizzas a good name.

Feel free to mix and match this chapter's doughs and finished pizza topping combinations. They're largely interchangeable.

Roman Cracker Dough

∽ MAKES ONE 11 X 14-INCH (28 X 36 CM) PIZZA ∽

Rome is home to several distinctive styles of pizza, one of which has an ultrathin, cracker-like base. This gluten-free version—uniformly flattened using a rolling pin—achieves the impossible: a crust that is both thin and crispy like a cracker yet also still chewy and flavorful. Our favorite bits are the hollow air pockets that form during the critical par-bake.

Tip: Par-baking the dough right after you've mixed the dough and pressed it out generates the most and biggest air bubble blisters. The longer the dough sits, the less dramatic the effect.

150 grams warm water (110°F/45°C)

1½ teaspoons sugar

1 teaspoon active dry yeast

50 grams brown rice flour

50 grams cornstarch

50 grams potato starch

12 grams millet flour

1 teaspoon ground psyllium husk

1 teaspoon salt

1 teaspoon xanthan gum

1 tablespoon olive oil

High-altitude modification: not required.

1. In a small bowl, whisk together the water, sugar, and yeast. Set aside to allow the yeast to activate, about 5 minutes, until foamy.

2. In a medium bowl, whisk together the rice flour, cornstarch, potato starch, millet flour, psyllium husk, salt, and xanthan gum.

3. When the yeast mixture is foamy on top, add the oil and stir to combine.

4. Pour the yeast mixture into the flour mixture and stir vigorously with a spoon until it is smooth, there are no lumps, and it forms a stiff, thick dough.

Prosciutto and Arugula

This flavor combo is a family favorite. In fact, we competed with a pizza just like this at the 2018 Caputo Cup pizza competition in New Jersey. Unlike many Italian and American pizzerias, which add the prosciutto after the pizza comes out of the oven, we parcook the prosciutto and add it to the pizza before the bake, so that it gets crispy, with an intensified, salty flavor.

1½ tablespoons olive oil, plus more for brushing the dough

2 garlic cloves, minced

¼ teaspoon red pepper flakes

4 ounces (115 g) thinly sliced prosciutto di Parma

1 prepared Roman Cracker Dough (page 66)

Bench flour (page 10)

½ cup (115 g) puréed canned San Marzano tomatoes

4 ounces (115 g) shredded low-moisture mozzarella

2 ounces (55 g) fresh mozzarella

1 handful baby arugula

1. Set your oven rack in the middle position and place your baking steel on it. Preheat the oven to 550°F (285°C) for at least 1 hour.

2. While the oven is preheating, combine 1 tablespoon of the oil, the garlic, and the red pepper flakes in a small bowl. Set aside.

3. Heat ½ tablespoon of the oil in a sauté pan over medium heat. Tear the prosciutto into pieces and add to the pan, tossing periodically until it starts to brown at the edges. Set aside.

4. To shape the dough, place an unfloured 15-inch (38 cm) square piece of parchment paper on a flat surface.

5. Using a spatula, scrape the dough onto the center of the parchment. With floured hands, press the dough into a flattened rectangle.

6. Dust the surface of the dough and a rolling pin with bench flour. Roll into a thin 11 x 14-inch (28 x 36 cm) rectangle (about ⅛ inch/3 mm thick), adding just enough flour to prevent sticking (see page 21 for technique tips).

7. Use a pizza wheel or sharp knife to trim away any jagged, uneven edges, leaving a smooth, finished edge with slightly rounded corners.

8. To par-bake the crust, brush the top of the dough with a thin coat of oil from edge to edge. Immediately use a lightly floured pizza peel to launch the dough-on-parchment onto the baking steel in the oven. Bake for 2 minutes.

9. Remove the dough-on-parchment from the oven and transfer to your kitchen counter. Generously dust the pizza peel with more flour, especially along the leading edge of the peel, then slide the peel between the parchment and the crust so that only the crust is directly on the peel.

10. To finish the pizza, ladle the tomatoes onto the crust and spread into an even layer, leaving a ½-inch (13 mm) border without any sauce. Sprinkle on the shredded mozzarella. Tear the fresh mozzarella into small pieces and place them on top, then add the prosciutto. Use a small spoon to drizzle the minced garlic in oil onto the pizza.

11. Return the pizza to the baking steel in the oven and bake for 4 to 5 minutes, until the edges of the crust are starting to turn deep golden brown but not burned.

12. Remove the pizza from the oven and transfer to a large cutting board. Scatter the arugula over the pizza. Let set for 2 minutes, then slice and serve hot.

Potato, Pancetta, and Rosemary

MAKES ONE 11 X 14-INCH (28 X 36 CM) PIZZA

During our gluten-free pizza research in Rome, we discovered a true diamond in the rough that you'd surely miss as a tourist: Pizzeria Teresina. Located in a residential corner of the city north of the Vatican, it's exclusively a takeaway window with scooter delivery within a tiny four-kilometer radius. It's actually two identical side-by-side pizzerias, one of which is dedicated gluten-free. When we asked them to make their signature pizza for us, this is the flavor combo they delivered, and we were duly impressed.

1 tablespoon olive oil, plus more for brushing the dough

2 ounces (55 g) finely diced pancetta

2 baby Yukon gold or red potatoes, sliced into ⅛-inch (3 mm) slices

1 shallot, halved and thinly sliced

1 garlic clove, minced

1 sprig rosemary, leaves removed from stalk and chopped (about 2 teaspoons)

⅛ teaspoon salt

⅛ teaspoon ground black pepper

1 prepared Roman Cracker Dough (page 66)

Bench flour (page 10)

4 ounces (115 g) shredded low-moisture mozzarella

2 ounces (55 g) fresh mozzarella

1. Set your oven rack in the middle position and place your baking steel on it. Preheat the oven to 550°F (285°C) for at least 1 hour.

2. **While the oven is preheating,** heat the oil in a large sauté pan over medium-high heat. Add the pancetta, tossing periodically until it begins to brown but is not crispy. Remove with a slotted spoon, leaving the oil behind.

3. Add the potatoes to the pan and sauté until they begin to soften, about 5 minutes. Add the shallot, garlic, rosemary, salt, and pepper and sauté until the shallot begins to soften, about 1 minute.

4. **To shape the dough,** place an unfloured 15-inch (38 cm) square piece of parchment paper on a flat surface.

5. Using a spatula, scrape the dough onto the center of the parchment. With floured hands, press the dough into a flattened rectangle.

6. Dust the surface of the dough and a rolling pin with bench flour. Roll into a thin 11 x 14-inch (28 x 36 cm) rectangle (about ⅛ inch/3 mm thick), adding just enough flour to prevent sticking (see page 21 for technique tips).

7. Use a pizza wheel or sharp knife to trim away any jagged, uneven edges, leaving a smooth, finished edge with slightly rounded corners.

8. **To par-bake the crust,** brush the top of the dough with a thin coat of oil from edge to edge. Immediately use a lightly floured pizza peel to launch the dough-on-parchment onto the baking steel in the oven. Bake for 2 minutes.

9. Remove the dough-on-parchment from the oven and transfer to your kitchen counter. Generously dust the pizza peel with more flour, especially along the leading edge of the peel, then slide the peel between the parchment and the crust, so that only the crust is directly on the peel.

10. **To finish the pizza,** sprinkle on the shredded mozzarella, leaving a 1-inch (2.5 cm) border around the edge. Tear the fresh mozzarella into small pieces and place them on top. Evenly distribute the potato mixture and pancetta across the top of the pizza.

11. Return the pizza to the baking steel in the oven and bake for 4 to 5 minutes, until the edges of the crust are starting to turn deep golden brown but not burned.

12. Remove the pizza from the oven and transfer to a large cutting board. Let set for 2 minutes, then slice and serve hot.

Spinach and Feta

⦿ MAKES ONE 11 X 14-INCH (28 X 36 CM) PIZZA ⦿

This quintessentially Greek combination of flavors can be found everywhere from spanakopita to pasta to quiche. And now, on your gluten-free pizza, too!

1 tablespoon olive oil, plus more for brushing the dough

1 garlic clove, minced

6 ounces (170 g) baby spinach leaves

2 green onions, chopped

⅛ teaspoon salt

⅛ teaspoon ground black pepper

1 prepared Roman Cracker Dough (page 66)

Bench flour (page 10)

4 ounces (115 g) crumbled feta

2 tablespoons grated Parmesan

1. Set your oven rack in the middle position and place your baking steel on it. Preheat the oven to 550°F (285°C) for at least 1 hour.

2. While the oven is preheating, heat the oil in a large sauté pan over medium-high heat. Add the garlic, sautéing until fragrant, about 30 seconds. Add the spinach and green onion, season with salt and pepper, and cook until the spinach releases its liquid. Transfer the mixture into a colander, gently pressing on the spinach to squeeze out excess liquid, and set aside, allowing any remaining liquid to drain off.

3. To shape the dough, place an unfloured 15-inch (38 cm) square piece of parchment paper on a flat surface.

4. Using a spatula, scrape the dough onto the center of the parchment. With floured hands, press the dough into a flattened rectangle.

5. Dust the surface of the dough and a rolling pin with bench flour. Roll into a thin 11 x 14-inch (28 x 36 cm) rectangle (about ⅛ inch/3 mm thick), adding just enough flour to prevent sticking (see page 21 for technique tips).

6. Use a pizza wheel or sharp knife to trim away any jagged, uneven edges, leaving a smooth, finished edge with slightly rounded corners.

7. To par-bake the crust, brush the top of the dough with a thin coat of oil from edge to edge. Immediately use a lightly floured pizza peel to launch the dough-on-parchment onto the baking steel in the oven. Bake for 2 minutes.

8. Remove the dough-on-parchment from the oven and transfer to your kitchen counter. Generously dust the pizza peel with more flour, especially along the leading edge of the peel, then slide the peel between the parchment and the crust, so that just the crust is directly on the peel.

9. To finish the pizza, distribute the spinach and feta over the crust, leaving a 1-inch (2.5 cm) border around the edge.

10. Return the pizza to the baking steel in the oven and bake for 4 to 5 minutes, until the edges of the crust are starting to turn deep golden brown but not burned.

11. Remove the pizza from the oven and transfer to a large cutting board. Sprinkle the Parmesan over the top. Let set for 2 minutes, then slice and serve hot.

Pear, Pecan, and Blue Cheese

MAKES ONE 11 X 14-INCH (28 X 36 CM) PIZZA

The salty creaminess of blue cheese, crunch from chopped pecans, sweetness from pears, and freshness from a finishing touch of baby arugula make this a winning combo.

1 prepared Roman Cracker Dough (page 66)

Bench flour (page 10)

Olive oil, for brushing the dough

1 ripe Bartlett pear, peeled, cored, and thinly sliced

4 ounces (115 g) crumbled blue cheese (double-check gluten-free status)

¼ cup (55 g) chopped pecans

1 handful baby arugula

2 tablespoons Balsamic Glaze (page 131)

1. Set your oven rack in the middle position and place your baking steel on it. Preheat the oven to 550°F (285°C) for at least 1 hour.

2. To shape the dough, place an unfloured 15-inch (38 cm) square piece of parchment paper on a flat surface.

3. Using a spatula, scrape the dough onto the center of the parchment. With floured hands, press the dough into a flattened rectangle.

4. Dust the surface of the dough and a rolling pin with bench flour. Roll into a thin 11 x 14-inch (28 x 36 cm) rectangle (about ⅛ inch/3 mm thick), adding just enough flour to prevent sticking (see page 21 for technique tips).

5. Use a pizza wheel or sharp knife to trim away any jagged, uneven edges, leaving a smooth, finished edge with slightly rounded corners.

6. To par-bake the crust, brush the top of the dough with a thin coat of oil from edge to edge. Immediately use a lightly floured pizza peel to launch the dough-on-parchment onto the baking steel in the oven. Bake for 2 minutes.

7. Remove the dough-on-parchment from the oven and transfer to your kitchen counter. Generously dust the pizza peel with more flour, especially along the leading edge of the peel, then slide the peel between the parchment and the crust, so that just the crust is directly on the peel.

8. To finish the pizza, arrange the sliced pear on the crust, leaving a 1-inch (2.5 cm) border around the edge. Sprinkle the blue cheese and pecans over the pear.

9. Return the pizza to the baking steel in the oven and bake for 4 to 5 minutes, until the edges of the crust are starting to turn deep golden brown but not burned.

10. Remove the pizza from the oven and transfer to a large cutting board. Top with arugula and drizzle with Balsamic Glaze. Let set for 2 minutes, then slice and serve hot.

Tavern Dough

From New Jersey bar pie, to Chicago tavern-style pizza, to St. Louis–style thin crust, this is America's answer to the Roman-style thin-crust pizza. It's ultrathin and often has the tomato sauce, cheese, and toppings added all the way to the edge, without leaving a border. Our gluten-free version takes the Roman-style cracker dough and gives it a 48-hour ferment.

150 grams warm water (110°F/45°C)

1½ teaspoons sugar

½ teaspoon active dry yeast

50 grams brown rice flour

50 grams cornstarch

50 grams potato starch

12 grams millet flour

1 teaspoon ground psyllium husk

1 teaspoon salt

1 teaspoon xanthan gum

1 tablespoon olive oil, plus more for greasing

High-altitude modification: not required.

1. In a small bowl, whisk together the water, sugar, and yeast. Set aside to allow the yeast to activate, about 5 minutes, until foamy.

2. In a medium bowl, whisk together the rice flour, cornstarch, potato starch, millet flour, psyllium husk, salt, and xanthan gum.

3. When the yeast mixture is foamy on top, add the oil and stir to combine.

4. Pour the yeast mixture into the flour mixture and stir vigorously with a spoon until it is smooth, there are no lumps, and it forms a stiff, thick dough.

5. Lightly grease a medium-sized container (glass or plastic) with oil. Place the dough in the container and loosely cover. (If the container has a lid, place the lid squarely on top of the container but do *not* snap it tightly shut. This allows excess carbon dioxide from the fermentation to escape, while preventing the dough from drying out. Otherwise, covering the container with a plate or loosely with plastic wrap works well.)

6. Refrigerate for 48 hours.

7. At least 2 hours before you plan to make pizza, remove the container from the refrigerator to allow the dough to come to room temperature.

Campari Margherita

Like any good margherita pizza, this gluten-free version is a testament to using a few fresh, quality ingredients to make something wonderfully delicious. Don't let the simplicity of the recipe fool you. The finished pizza pays great dividends, and your taste buds will thank you. Unlike our gluten-free Neapolitan Margherita with its puréed San Marzano tomatoes, this tavern version opts for sliced fresh Campari tomatoes. (Do feel free to substitute your favorite garden-fresh heirloom variety of tomato. We certainly do when our backyard garden offers up ripe tomatoes in the summertime!)

Light olive oil, for shaping and brushing the dough

1 prepared Tavern Dough (page 77)

Bench flour (page 10)

4 Campari tomatoes, thinly sliced

5 ounces (140 g) fresh mozzarella

10 basil leaves, chiffonade

Generous pinch coarse kosher salt

Extra virgin olive oil

1. Set your oven rack in the middle position and place your baking steel on it. Preheat the oven to 550°F (285°C) for at least 1 hour.

2. To shape the dough, place an unfloured 15-inch (38 cm) square piece of parchment paper on a flat surface.

3. Generously coat the palms of your hands with light olive oil. Using a spatula, scrape the dough out of the container and into your hands. While holding the dough, form it into a smooth ball.

4. Place the dough onto the center of the parchment. With oiled hands, press the dough into a flattened rectangle.

5. Using an oiled rolling pin, roll the dough into an 11 x 14-inch (28 x 36 cm) rectangle (about ⅛ inch/3 mm thick), adding additional oil to the rolling pin as needed to prevent sticking (see page 21 for technique tips).

6. Use a pizza wheel or sharp knife to trim away any jagged, uneven edges, leaving a smooth, finished edge with slightly rounded corners.

7. To par-bake the crust, brush the top of the dough with a thin coat of light olive oil from edge to edge. Use a lightly floured pizza peel to launch the dough-on-parchment onto the baking steel in the oven. Bake for 2 minutes.

8. Remove the dough-on-parchment from the oven and transfer to your kitchen counter. Generously dust the pizza peel with more flour, especially along the leading edge of the peel, then slide the peel between the parchment and the crust, so that only the crust is directly on the peel.

9. Distribute the tomatoes on the crust. Tear the mozzarella into small pieces and place them on top.

10. Return the pizza to the baking steel in the oven and bake for 4 to 5 minutes, until the edges of the crust are starting to turn golden brown but not burned.

11. Remove the pizza from the oven and transfer to a large cutting board. Sprinkle the basil and salt over the pizza. Then drizzle lightly with extra virgin olive oil. Let set for 2 minutes, then slice and serve hot.

Mushrooms and Sun-Dried Tomatoes

MAKES ONE 11 X 14-INCH (28 X 36 CM) PIZZA

This pizza is earthy . . . in a good way! The sautéed mushrooms have their flavor boosted by a splash of vermouth, while the sun-dried tomatoes and fresh basil add a Mediterranean touch.

Ingredients

1 tablespoon light olive oil, plus more for shaping and brushing the dough

1 garlic clove, minced

4 ounces (115 g) cremini mushrooms, thinly sliced

⅛ teaspoon salt

⅛ teaspoon ground black pepper

2 tablespoons vermouth

1 prepared Tavern Dough (page 77)

Bench flour (page 10)

½ cup (115 g) puréed canned San Marzano tomatoes

6 ounces (170 g) shredded low-moisture mozzarella

¼ cup (55 g) drained, sliced sun-dried tomatoes

10 basil leaves, chiffonade

2 teaspoons grated Parmesan

Extra virgin olive oil

---

1. Set your oven rack in the middle position and place your baking steel on it. Preheat the oven to 550°F (285°C) for at least 1 hour.

2. While the oven is preheating, heat the light olive oil in a large sauté pan over medium heat. Add the garlic and heat until fragrant, about 30 seconds.

3. Add the mushrooms, season with salt and pepper, and continue to cook until they release their liquid, about 3 minutes.

4. Add the vermouth and continue to cook until all of the moisture has evaporated and/or reabsorbed into the mushrooms, about 2 minutes. Set aside.

5. To shape the dough, place an unfloured 15-inch (38 cm) square piece of parchment paper on a flat surface.

6. Generously coat the palms of your hands with light olive oil. Using a spatula, scrape the dough out of the container and into your hands. While holding the dough, form it into a smooth ball.

7. Place the dough onto the center of the parchment. With oiled hands, press the dough into a flattened rectangle.

8. Using an oiled rolling pin, roll the dough into a thin 11 x 14-inch (28 x 36 cm) rectangle (about ⅛ inch/3 mm thick), adding additional oil to the rolling pin as needed to prevent sticking (see page 21 for technique tips).

9. Use a pizza wheel or sharp knife to trim away any jagged, uneven edges, leaving a smooth, finished edge with slightly rounded corners.

10. To par-bake the crust, brush the top of the dough with a thin coat of light olive oil from edge to edge. Use a lightly floured pizza peel to launch the dough-on-parchment onto the baking steel in the oven. Bake for 2 minutes.

11. Remove the dough-on-parchment from the oven and transfer to your kitchen counter. Generously dust the pizza peel with more flour, especially along the leading edge of the peel, then slide the peel between the parchment and the crust, so that just the crust is directly on the peel.

12. To finish the pizza, spread the puréed tomatoes over the surface of the crust. Distribute the mozzarella over the sauce, then top with the mushrooms and sun-dried tomatoes.

13. Return the pizza to the baking steel in the oven and bake for 4 to 5 minutes, until the edges of the crust are starting to turn golden brown but not burned.

14. Remove the pizza from the oven and transfer to a large cutting board. Sprinkle the basil and Parmesan over the pizza, then drizzle lightly with extra virgin olive oil. Let set for 2 minutes, then slice and serve hot.

Four Cheese al Taglio

⤳ MAKES ONE 8 X 14-INCH (20 X 36 CM) PIZZA ⤳

Alongside the Roman cracker crust, the al taglio pizza is one of Rome's other signature pizza styles, which has since become popular much farther afield in places such as New York and—new for 2019—a Roman competition division at the International Pizza Challenge in Las Vegas. Al taglio pizzas are long and rectangular and usually sold either by the slice or by weight. Our gluten-free version is based on our Neapolitan Dough but prepared differently to achieve the al taglio effect. This four-cheese version is a great intro.

1. Set your oven rack in the top position (3 to 4 inches [7.5 to 10 cm] below the oven's broiler elements) and place your baking steel on it. Preheat the oven to 550°F (285°C) for at least 45 minutes.

2. **After preheating,** make the Neapolitan Dough (page 55).

3. Immediately before shaping the dough, superheat the baking steel (page 22).

4. **To shape the dough,** place a 15-inch (38 cm) square piece of parchment paper on a flat surface. Dust about 2 teaspoons bench flour onto the parchment.

5. Using a spatula, scrape the dough out of the bowl onto the center of the parchment and smooth the surface of the dough.

6. Coat your hands with light olive oil. Carefully tease the dough into an 8 x 14-inch (20 x 36 cm) rectangle with rounded edges, adding additional oil to your hands if the dough sticks. The finished, pressed out dough should be very thin.

7. **To finish the pizza,** set the oven from broil back to bake at 550°F (285°C). (If you had the oven door ajar to keep the broiler firing, close the oven door now to trap heat.)

8. Brush the entire surface of the dough with the 2 tablespoons light olive oil, until the dough glistens but does not have any standing pools of oil.

9. Remove any extra flour from around the edge of the dough. Then use a lightly floured pizza peel to launch the dough-on-parchment onto the baking steel in the oven. Bake for 3 minutes.

10. Use the peel to remove the dough-on-parchment from the oven and transfer it to the kitchen counter. Lightly flour the peel and slide the crust onto the peel from the parchment.

11. Spread the cheeses over the surface of the crust.

12. Return the pizza to the oven directly on the steel and bake for 3 to 4 minutes, until the crust is deep golden brown.

13. Remove the pizza from the oven and transfer to a large cutting board. Place the basil leaves so that you have one basil leaf per slice. Finish with a drizzle of extra virgin olive oil. Let set for 2 minutes, then slice and serve hot.

---

1 recipe Neapolitan Dough (page 55; prepared *after* preheating the oven)

Bench flour (page 10)

2 tablespoons light olive oil, plus more for working and brushing the dough

2 ounces (55 g) shredded asiago

2 ounces (55 g) shredded fontina

2 ounces (55 g) fresh mozzarella, torn into pieces

2 tablespoons grated Parmesan

10 basil leaves

Extra virgin olive oil

Burrata and Roasted Red Pepper al Taglio

∽ MAKES ONE 8 X 14-INCH (20 X 36 CM) PIZZA ∾

The cream concealed within a ball of burrata cheese makes this pizza feel especially decadent, even though it's relatively simple. The roasted red peppers cut through that creaminess with a distinctly Mediterranean flare.

1 recipe Neapolitan Dough (page 55; prepared *after* preheating the oven)

Bench flour (page 10)

2 tablespoons light olive oil, plus more for working and brushing the dough

¼ cup (55 g) puréed canned San Marzano tomatoes

¼ cup (60 g) drained, sliced roasted red peppers

4 ounces (115 g) burrata

8 basil leaves

Extra virgin olive oil

Coarse kosher salt

1. Set your oven rack in the top position (3 to 4 inches [7.5 to 10 cm] below the oven's broiler elements) and place your baking steel on it. Preheat the oven to 550°F (285°C) for at least 45 minutes.

2. After preheating, make the Neapolitan Dough (page 55).

3. Immediately before shaping the dough, superheat the baking steel (page 22).

4. To shape the dough, place a 15-inch (38 cm) square piece of parchment paper on a flat surface. Dust about 2 teaspoons bench flour onto the parchment.

5. Using a spatula, scrape the dough out of the bowl onto the center of the parchment and smooth the dough.

6. Coat your palms and fingers with light olive oil. Carefully tease the dough into an 8 x 14-inch (20 x 36 cm) rectangle with rounded edges, adding additional oil to your hands if the dough sticks. The finished, pressed out dough should be very thin.

7. To finish the pizza, set the oven from broil back to bake at 550°F (285°C). (If you had the oven door ajar to keep

8. Brush the entire surface of the dough with the 2 tablespoons light olive oil, until the dough glistens but does not have any standing pools of oil.

9. Remove any extra flour from around the edge of the dough. Then use a lightly floured dough peel to launch the dough-on-parchment onto the baking steel in the oven. Bake for 3 minutes.

10. Use the peel to remove the dough-on-parchment from the oven and transfer it to the kitchen counter. Lightly flour the peel and slide the crust onto the peel from the parchment.

11. Spread the tomatoes and red peppers over the surface of the crust.

12. Return the pizza to the oven directly on the steel and bake for 3 to 4 minutes, until the crust is deep golden brown.

13. Remove the pizza from the oven and transfer to a large cutting board. Tear the burrata into pieces and place on top, then add the basil. Finish with a drizzle of extra virgin olive and a sprinkle of salt. Let set for 2 minutes, then slice and serve hot.

DEEP-DISH PAN PIZZAS

Chicago-style deep dish. Detroit-style pizza. Sicilian pizza. The grandma pie. Despite stylistic differences, they all share two things in common: 1) They're thick and/or deep, and 2) they're pizzas cooked at lower temperatures in pans of various shapes and sizes.

But gluten-free versions of these deep-dish and thick-crust pan pizzas are incredibly hard to find at pizzerias. Apart from a handful of glorious exceptions, the gluten-free option—if it's available at all—is still almost always a thin cracker crust.

They can also be particularly tricky to replicate with gluten-free flours. How can deep-dish pan pizzas hold their structure so that the crust is tall and puffy, while remaining light, with a moist interior that doesn't cross over into "gummy" territory?

Answer: this chapter's recipes.

> **Note:** Don't overmix these doughs. Overmixing can cause the thick-crust pizzas to collapse and lose some of their loft. Mix just until the ingredients are incorporated and the dough is smooth.

Chicago Deep-Dish Dough

~ MAKES ONE 9-INCH (23 CM) PIZZA ~

Chicago-style deep-dish pizza goes heavy on the toppings, with built-up layers of cheese, fillings, and sauce. Unique among pizza dough styles, it has a buttered crust. This gluten-free version should satisfy even the most die-hard Chicago fan.

155 grams warm water (110°F/45°C)

1½ teaspoons sugar

1 teaspoon active dry yeast

50 grams brown rice flour

50 grams cornstarch

50 grams potato starch

12 grams cornmeal

12 grams millet flour

1 teaspoon ground psyllium husk

1 teaspoon salt

1 teaspoon xanthan gum

3 tablespoons melted butter

Olive oil, for pressing out the dough

High-altitude modification: Increase the water to 175 grams.

1. In a small bowl, whisk together the water, sugar, and yeast. Set aside to allow the yeast to activate, about 5 minutes, until foamy.

2. In a medium bowl, whisk together the rice flour, cornstarch, potato starch, cornmeal, millet flour, psyllium husk, salt, and xanthan gum.

3. Pour 1 tablespoon of the butter into a 9-inch (23 cm) round nonstick cake pan. Use your fingers or a pastry brush to spread the butter over the bottom of the pan. Leave the sides clean.

4. When the yeast mixture is foamy on top, add the remaining 2 tablespoons butter and stir to combine. Pour the yeast mixture into the flour mixture and stir vigorously with a spoon until it is smooth, there are no lumps, and it forms a wet dough.

5. Use a spatula to scrape the dough into the prepared pan. Oil your hands and press the dough into a uniform layer on the bottom and 1½ inches (4 cm) up the sides of the pan. Set aside and allow to rise for 30 minutes.

Deep-Dish Mushroom, Pepper, and Onion

⮑ MAKES ONE 9-INCH (23 CM) PIZZA ⮐

If you like your Chicago-style deep-dish pizza loaded with veg, this is the recipe for you.

1 recipe Chicago Deep Dish Dough (page 88; prepared while the oven is preheating)

2 tablespoons olive oil

8 ounces (225 g) button mushrooms, sliced

¼ teaspoon salt

1 bell pepper, sliced

1 medium onion, sliced

4 ounces (115 g) thinly sliced provolone

6 ounces (170 g) shredded low-moisture mozzarella

1¼ cups (310 g) Marinara Sauce (page 155)

2 tablespoons grated Parmesan

1. Set your oven rack in the middle position and preheat the oven to 425°F (220°C).

2. While the oven is preheating, make the Chicago Deep-Dish Dough (page 88) and let it rise.

3. Meanwhile, heat the oil in a large sauté pan over medium-high heat. Add the mushrooms and salt and sauté until the liquid is released and has evaporated. Remove the mushrooms and set aside.

4. Add the pepper and onion to the pan, adding additional oil if needed. Sauté until soft, about 5 minutes. Return the mushrooms to the pan and toss to combine, then remove from the heat.

5. To finish the pizza, after the dough has risen for 30 minutes, layer the provolone to fully cover the bottom of the dough. Distribute the mozzarella on top. Distribute the vegetables over the cheese. Spread the Marinara Sauce over the vegetables and sprinkle the Parmesan on top.

6. Bake for 35 minutes, or until the crust is deep golden brown.

7. Remove from the oven and allow to cool for 5 minutes, then slice and serve hot.

Deep-Dish Sausage

With layers of provolone and mozzarella cheese, Italian sausage, and marinara sauce, this is an homage to the original Chicago-style deep-dish pizza that first came onto the scene in the 1940s.

1 recipe Chicago Deep-Dish Dough (page 88; prepared while preheating the oven)

4 ounces (115 g) thinly sliced provolone

6 ounces (170 g) shredded low-moisture mozzarella

5 ounces (140 g) Italian sausage, casings removed

1¼ cups (310 g) Marinara Sauce (page 155)

2 tablespoons grated Parmesan

1. Set your oven rack in the middle position and preheat the oven to 425°F (220°C).

2. While the oven is preheating, make the Chicago Deep-Dish Dough (page 88) and let it rise.

3. To finish the pizza, after the dough has risen for 30 minutes, layer the provolone to fully cover the bottom of the dough. Distribute the mozzarella on top. Break the sausage into small pieces and scatter it over the cheese. Spread the Marinara Sauce over the sausage and sprinkle the Parmesan on top.

4. Bake for 35 minutes, or until the crust is deep golden brown.

5. Remove from the oven and allow to cool for 5 minutes, then slice and serve hot.

Deep-Dish Pepperoni and Bacon

⤳ MAKES ONE 9-INCH (23 CM) PIZZA ⤳

Chicago-style pizza is known for going heavy on the meats. This pizza's pairing of pepperoni and smoky bacon hits the bull's-eye.

1 recipe Chicago Deep-Dish Dough (page 88; prepared while the oven is preheating)

8 slices bacon, cut into large pieces

4 ounces (115 g) thinly sliced provolone

6 ounces (170 g) shredded low-moisture mozzarella

4 ounces (115 g) small "coin" pepperoni

1¼ cups (310 g) Marinara Sauce (page 155)

2 tablespoons grated Parmesan

1. Set your oven rack in the middle position and preheat the oven to 425°F (220°C).

2. While the oven is preheating, make the Chicago Deep-Dish Dough (page 88) and let it rise.

3. Meanwhile, heat a medium sauté pan over medium-high heat. Add the bacon and cook until crispy. Remove from the pan. When cool enough to handle, crumble and set aside.

4. To finish the pizza, after the dough has risen for 30 minutes, layer the provolone to fully cover the bottom of the dough. Distribute the mozzarella on top. Distribute the pepperoni and then the bacon on top of the cheese. Spread the Marinara Sauce over the meat and sprinkle the Parmesan on top.

5. Bake for 35 minutes, or until the crust is deep golden brown.

6. Remove from the oven and allow to cool for 5 minutes, then slice and serve hot.

Deep-Dish Spinach and Ricotta

୬ MAKES ONE 9-INCH (23 CM) PIZZA ୬

Chicago-style deep-dish pizza isn't known for being light on the stomach.
But this spinach and ricotta version comes reasonably close.

1 recipe Chicago Deep-Dish Dough (page 88; prepared while preheating the oven)

1 tablespoon olive oil

2 garlic cloves, minced

8 ounces (225 g) baby spinach leaves

4 ounces (115 g) thinly sliced provolone

6 ounces (170 g) shredded low-moisture mozzarella

½ cup (115 g) Ricotta (page 202)

1¼ cups (310 g) Marinara Sauce (page 155)

2 tablespoons grated Parmesan

1. Set your oven rack in the middle position and preheat the oven to 425°F (220°C).

2. While the oven is preheating, make the Chicago Deep-Dish Dough (page 88) and let it rise.

3. Meawhile, heat the oil in a large sauté pan over medium-high heat. Add the garlic and stir until fragrant, about 30 seconds. Add the spinach and sauté until wilted. Transfer to a colander and press with a spatula to remove any extra moisture.

4. To finish the pizza, after the dough has risen for 30 minutes, layer the provolone to fully cover the bottom of the dough. Distribute the mozzarella on top. Spread the spinach over the cheese. Dollop the Ricotta onto the spinach. Spread the Marinara Sauce over the spinach and Ricotta and sprinkle the Parmesan on top.

5. Bake for 35 minutes, or until the crust is deep golden brown.

6. Remove from the oven and allow to cool for 5 minutes, then slice and serve hot.

Sicilian Dough

Chicago-style pizza may get deep, but Sicilian takes the cake for thickest crust. Especially popular in the New York City metro area where there's a strong Italian American population, a good square of Sicilian should be thick but still light and airy. Like traditional Sicilian pizzas, our gluten-free version gets a long rise time and par-bake in order to achieve a pillowy crust. Whether you're a corner or an edge person, grab a square and enjoy.

450 grams warm water (110°F/45°C)

1 tablespoon plus 1 teaspoon sugar

1 tablespoon plus 2 teaspoons active dry yeast

194 grams white rice flour

106 grams quinoa flour

94 grams tapioca starch

81 grams potato starch

18 grams (about 5 teaspoons) ground psyllium husk

12 grams (about 2 teaspoons) salt

4 tablespoons olive oil, plus more for pressing out the dough

High-altitude modification: Increase the water to 500 grams and decrease the yeast to 1 tablespoon plus 1 teaspoon.

1. In a small bowl, whisk together the water, sugar, and yeast. Set aside to allow the yeast to activate, about 5 minutes, until foamy.

2. In a medium bowl, whisk together the rice flour, quinoa flour, tapioca starch, potato starch, psyllium husk, and salt.

3. When the yeast mixture is foamy on top, add 3 tablespoons of the oil and stir to combine.

4. Add the yeast mixture to the flours and stir vigorously until completely smooth. If using an electric mixer, mix only until the dough is smooth. Do not overmix.

5. With the remaining tablespoon oil, grease a well-seasoned or nonstick quarter sheet pan.

6. Use a spatula to scrape the dough into the prepared pan, then oil your hands and press the dough down evenly until it reaches into the corners of the pan. Avoid small pools of oil on top of the dough, as they will inhibit the rise.

7. Set the dough in a warm place, cover with an inverted cake pan, and leave to rise for 2 hours. (The dough will rise higher than the lip of the quarter sheet pan. Make sure the inverted cake pan leaves enough headroom so it doesn't touch the risen dough.)

Grandma Dough

Invented by legendary pizzaiolo Ciro Cesarano of King Umberto in Elmont, New York, the grandma pie is a close cousin of the Sicilian. The dough is similar and also baked in rectangular pans, but the grandma pie's crust has less height than the lofty Sicilian's. Thanks to the oiled pan, a good grandma pie has a crispy exterior, even though the interior remains moist and light.

288 grams warm water (110°F/45°C)

2½ teaspoons sugar

3 teaspoons active dry yeast

125 grams white rice flour

68 grams quinoa flour

60 grams tapioca starch

52 grams potato starch

1 tablespoon ground psyllium husk

1 teaspoon salt

3 tablespoons olive oil, plus more for pressing out the dough

High-altitude modification: Increase the water to 320 grams and decrease the yeast to 2½ teaspoons.

1. In a small bowl, whisk together the water, sugar, and yeast. Set aside to allow the yeast to activate, about 5 minutes, until foamy.

2. In a medium bowl, whisk together the rice flour, quinoa flour, tapioca starch, potato starch, psyllium husk, and salt.

3. When the yeast mixture is foamy on top, add 2 tablespoons of the oil and stir to combine.

4. Add the yeast mixture to the flours and stir vigorously until completely smooth. If using an electric mixer, mix only until the dough is smooth. Do not overmix.

5. With the remaining tablespoon of oil, grease a well-seasoned or nonstick quarter sheet pan.

6. Use a spatula to scrape the dough into the prepared pan, then oil your hands and press the dough down evenly until it reaches into the corners of the pan. Avoid small pools of oil on top of the dough, as they will inhibit the rise.

7. Set in a warm place, cover, and leave to rise for 90 minutes.

Upside-Down Red Top

⁓ MAKES 1 QUARTER-SHEET-PAN PIZZA (9 X 13 INCHES/23 X 33 CM) ⁓

With an uncooked San Marzano tomato sauce on top of sliced mozzarella cheese, this upside-down pizza bursts with tomato flavor and is the traditional standard pie for many Long Island pizzerias.

1 prepared Sicilian Dough (page 99) or Grandma Dough (page 100)

6 ounces (170 g) low-moisture mozzarella, sliced

½ cup (115 g) puréed canned San Marzano tomatoes

2 teaspoons dried basil

2 teaspoons dried oregano

1. Set your oven rack in the middle position and preheat the oven to 300°F (150°C).

2. Par-bake the risen dough for 60 minutes for a Sicilian pizza or 40 minutes for a grandma pie. Then remove from the oven, leaving the crust in the pan.

3. Increase the oven temperature to 450°F (230°C).

4. To finish the pizza, spread the mozzarella on top of the crust, nearly to the edge of the pan. Ladle the tomatoes on top of the cheese and spread until just shy of the edge of the cheese. Sprinkle the basil and oregano on top of the sauce.

5. Return the pizza to the oven and bake for 10 minutes.

6. Remove from the oven and use a spatula to de-pan and help transfer the pizza onto a large cutting board. Allow to cool for 5 minutes, then cut and serve.

A la Vodka

When King Umberto pizzaiolo Giovanni Cesarano—
son of legendary pizza maker Ciro Cesarano and a highly
respected pizza maker himself—won the gluten-free division
of the prestigious 2018 Caputo Cup, he did it with a Sicilian pie
topped with vodka sauce. We don't have his secret recipe,
but the idea and the flavors were too good not to honor him
with a version of our own.

1 prepared Sicilian
Dough (page 99)
or Grandma Dough
(page 100)

1 cup (300 g) Vodka
Sauce (page 105)

6 ounces (170 g)
shredded low-
moisture mozzarella

2 tablespoons grated
Parmesan

10 fresh basil leaves,
chiffonade

1. Set your oven rack in the middle position
and preheat the oven to 300°F (150°C).

2. Par-bake the risen dough for 60 minutes
for a Sicilian pizza or 40 minutes for a
grandma pie. Then remove from the oven,
leaving the crust in the pan.

3. Increase the oven temperature to 450°F
(230°C).

4. To finish the pizza, ladle ½ cup (150 g)
of the Vodka Sauce on top of the crust,
spreading almost all the way to the edge, and
sprinkle the mozzarella on top.

5. Return the pizza to the oven and bake for
15 minutes.

6. Remove from the oven and use a spatula
to de-pan and help transfer the pizza onto a
large cutting board.

7. Ladle the remaining sauce onto the cooked
pizza in diagonal stripes. Then sprinkle
the Parmesan evenly over the entire pizza.
Garnish, scattering the basil between the
stripes of Vodka Sauce.

8. Allow to cool for 5 minutes, then cut
and serve.

Vodka Sauce

MAKES 2½ CUPS (750 G)

1 teaspoon olive oil

3 slices bacon, diced

1 medium onion, halved and thinly sliced

2 garlic cloves, minced

2 tablespoons vodka

One 14.5-ounce (411 g) can crushed or diced tomatoes

½ cup (120 ml) heavy cream

½ teaspoon dried basil

½ teaspoon red pepper flakes

¼ teaspoon salt

¼ teaspoon ground black pepper

1. Heat the oil in a medium saucepan over medium-high heat. Sauté the bacon until it begins to crisp. Decrease the heat to medium, then add the onions and garlic. Sauté until the onions are translucent and very soft, about 10 minutes.

2. Add the vodka to deglaze the pan and cook for 2 minutes. Add the tomatoes and simmer for 5 minutes. Purée the sauce with a handheld immersion blender until almost smooth (or transfer to a traditional blender and then return the mixture to the saucepan).

3. Add the cream, basil, and red pepper flakes and simmer for 5 minutes. Season with the salt and pepper and set aside. The sauce can be used immediately or stored in an airtight container in the refrigerator for up to 1 week.

Pepperoni

This pizza is all about the 'roni cups—when small "coin" pepperoni curl upwards in the heat of the oven, each containing a small bit of flavorful pepperoni oil.

1 prepared Sicilian Dough (page 99) or Grandma Dough (page 100)

½ cup (115 g) puréed canned San Marzano tomatoes

6 ounces (170 g) shredded low-moisture mozzarella

2 ounces (55 g) spicy small "coin" pepperoni

1 teaspoon dried basil

1 teaspoon dried oregano

1. Set your oven rack in the middle position and preheat the oven to 300°F (150°C).

2. Par-bake the risen dough for 60 minutes for a Sicilian pizza or 40 minutes for a grandma pie. Then remove from the oven, leaving the crust in the pan.

3. Increase the oven temperature to 450°F (230°C).

4. To finish the pizza, ladle the tomatoes on top of the crust, spreading almost all the way to the edge, and sprinkle the mozzarella on top. Scatter the pepperoni on top, then sprinkle on the basil and oregano.

5. Return the pizza to the oven and bake for 15 minutes, until the edges of the pepperoni start to crisp.

6. Remove from the oven and use a spatula to de-pan and help transfer the pizza onto a large cutting board. Allow to cool for 5 minutes, then cut and serve.

Broccoli Rabe and Sausage

The mild bitterness of the broccoli rabe and spicy sweetness of the sausage pair beautifully on this pizza. This meat and veg combo gives prosciutto and arugula a run for its money!

1 prepared Sicilian Dough (page 99) or Grandma Dough (page 100)

½ bunch (about 225 g) broccoli rabe

1 tablespoon light olive oil

1 garlic clove, minced

⅛ teaspoon red pepper flakes

4 ounces (115 g) Italian sausage, casings removed

½ cup (115 g) puréed canned San Marzano tomatoes

6 ounces (170 g) shredded low-moisture mozzarella

2 tablespoons grated Pecorino Romano

1 tablespoon extra virgin olive oil

1. Set your oven rack in the middle position and preheat the oven to 300°F (150°C).

2. Par-bake the risen dough for 60 minutes for a Sicilian pizza or 40 minutes for a grandma pie.

3. While the crust is baking, bring a large pot of salted water to a boil and fill a large bowl with ice water.

4. Trim the bottom inch (2.5 cm) off the broccoli rabe, then add to the boiling water. Boil for 3 minutes, then submerge in ice water to stop the cooking process. Transfer to a towel to dry.

5. Heat the light olive oil in a large sauté pan over medium-high heat. Add the garlic and red pepper flakes, sautéing until the garlic is fragrant, about 30 seconds. Add the broccoli rabe, toss to coat with the oil, and cook until just tender, about 5 minutes. Remove from the pan. When the broccoli rabe is cool, cut into 1-inch (2.5 cm) segments.

6. In the same sauté pan, add the sausage and cook until browned, about 5 minutes.

7. After par-baking, remove the crust from the oven, leaving it in the pan. Increase the oven temperature to 450°F (230°C).

8. To finish the pizza, ladle the tomatoes on top of the crust, spreading almost all the way to the edge, and sprinkle the mozzarella on top. Place the broccoli rabe and sausage on top, and sprinkle with the Pecorino Romano.

9. Return the pizza to the oven and bake for 15 minutes, until the cheese is starting to turn golden brown in places.

10. Remove from the oven and use a spatula to de-pan and help transfer the pizza onto a large cutting board. Drizzle with extra virgin olive oil. Allow to cool for 5 minutes, then cut and serve.

Detroit Dough

∽ MAKES ONE 9-INCH (23 CM) SQUARE PIZZA ∽

Like its cousins, the Sicilian and grandma pies, the Detroit-style pizza is
thick and baked in seasoned, oiled, square or rectangular pans. One of its
defining elements is a crowning rim of crisp, caramelized
mozzarella cheese around the edge.

245 grams warm water (110°F/45°C)

2 teaspoons sugar

2½ teaspoons active dry yeast

106 grams white rice flour

58 grams quinoa flour

51 grams tapioca starch

44 grams potato starch

2½ teaspoons ground psyllium husk

¾ teaspoon salt

3 tablespoons olive oil, plus more for pressing out the dough

High-altitude modification: Increase the water to 272 grams and decrease the yeast to 2 teaspoons.

1. In a small bowl, whisk together the water, sugar, and yeast. Set aside to allow the yeast to activate, about 5 minutes, until foamy.

2. In a medium bowl, whisk together the rice flour, quinoa flour, tapioca starch, potato starch, psyllium husk, and salt.

3. When the yeast mixture is foamy on top, add 2 tablespoons of the oil and stir to combine.

4. Add the yeast mixture to the flours and stir vigorously just until it is completely smooth. If you use an electric mixer, mix only until the dough is smooth. Do not overmix.

5. Grease a well-seasoned or nonstick 9-inch (23 cm) square pan with the remaining tablespoon oil.

6. Use a spatula to scrape the dough into the prepared pan, then oil your hands and press the dough evenly into the pan until it reaches into the corners. Avoid small pools of oil on top of the dough, as they will inhibit the rise.

7. Set in a warm place, cover, and leave to rise for 90 minutes.

Square Cheese

With tomato sauce under the cheese, and bright red dollops of tomato on top of the cheese as well, this classic take on the Detroit is a beauty.

1 prepared Detroit Dough (page 110)

¾ cup (170 g) puréed canned San Marzano tomatoes

8 ounces (225 g) shredded low-moisture mozzarella

½ teaspoon dried basil

½ teaspoon dried oregano

1. Set your oven rack in the middle position and preheat the oven to 300°F (150°C).

2. Par-bake the risen dough for 40 minutes. Then remove from the oven, leaving the crust in the pan.

3. Increase the oven temperature to 450°F (230°C).

4. To finish the pizza, ladle ½ cup (115 g) of the tomatoes onto the crust and spread to the edge of the pan. Sprinkle a thin layer of mozzarella on top of the tomatoes. Use the remaining mozzarella to build a border around the edge directly up against the metal walls of the pan. (Take care not to burn your fingers on the hot pan.) Sprinkle on the basil and oregano. Add the remaining tomatoes in small dollops on top.

5. Return the pizza to the oven and bake for 15 minutes, until the rim of mozzarella is well-caramelized.

6. Remove from the oven and use a spatula to de-pan and help transfer the pizza onto a large cutting board. Allow to cool for 5 minutes, then cut and serve.

GRILLED
PIZZAS

There's nothing like the smoky char—and signature grill marks—of a grilled pizza. Whether your fuel of choice is gas, propane, lump charcoal, or briquettes, this chapter's grilled pizzas will wow your taste buds and have you firing up the grill, even in the dead of winter.

Because the gluten-free dough starts wetter than conventional wheat-based dough, it requires a brief par-bake in the oven so that the pizza doesn't stick to the grill—or worse, fall through the grate! After the short par-bake, the rest of the pizza action happens out on the grill.

The result is the closest thing to a flame-kissed pizza you can get, short of installing a wood-fired pizza oven in the backyard. This chapter includes two doughs: a quick version and a 48-hour fermented version.

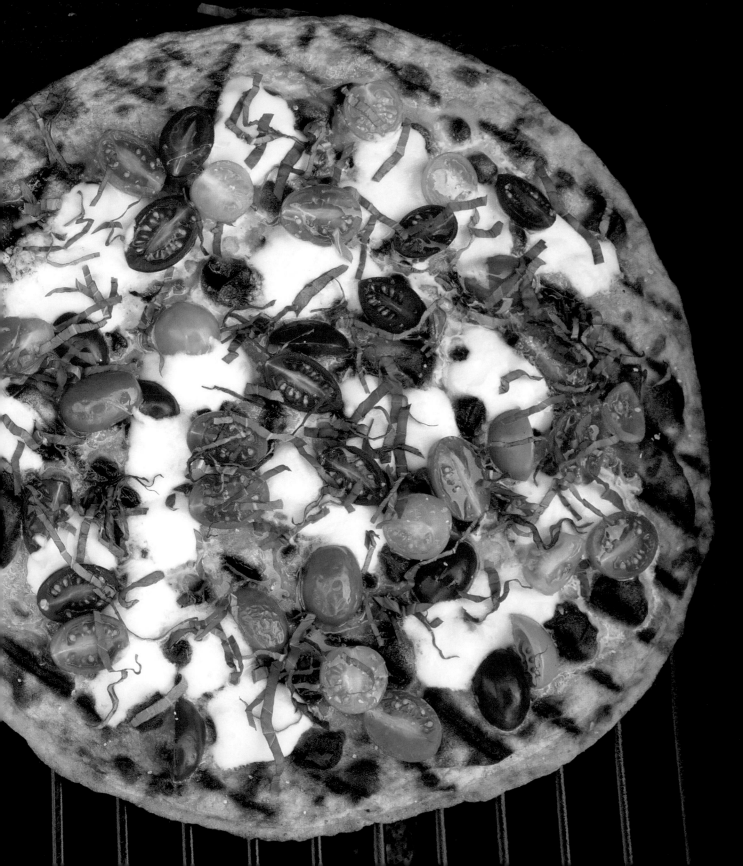

Grilled Dough

Quick Version

∽ MAKES ONE 12- TO 13-INCH (33 CM) PIZZA ∽

A grilled crust achieves a fire-roasted char that you simply can't get with an oven. This quick version of the dough has a leg up on its fermented sibling: It blisters with oodles of big air pockets and gets bold grill marks on both sides. It's gorgeous.

225 grams warm water (110°F/45°C)

1½ teaspoons sugar

1 teaspoon active dry yeast

75 grams quinoa flour

50 grams potato starch

50 grams tapioca starch

12 grams coconut flour

1 teaspoon ground psyllium husk

1 teaspoon xanthan gum

¾ teaspoon salt

1 tablespoon olive oil

High-altitude modification: Increase the water to 250 grams.

1. In a small bowl, whisk together the water, sugar, and yeast. Set aside to allow the yeast to activate, about 5 minutes, until foamy.

2. In a medium bowl, whisk together the quinoa flour, potato starch, tapioca starch, coconut flour, psyllium husk, xanthan gum, and salt.

3. When the yeast mixture is foamy on top, add the oil and stir to combine.

4. Pour the yeast mixture into the flour mixture and stir vigorously with a spoon until it is smooth, thickens slightly, and forms a loose dough. It should be very sticky and too wet to hold.

Tip: Par-baking the dough right after you've mixed and pressed it out generates the most and biggest blisters. The longer the dough sits, the less dramatic the effect.

Grilled Dough
48-Hour Fermentation

Though their ingredients are identical down to the very last drop of water, the fermented and quick grilled doughs are quite different. The fermented dough doesn't develop the same dramatic blistering, but we keep coming back for a few reasons: It tastes superior, it's more digestible, and it's just plain easy to eat. Whole pizzas disappear before we've had a chance to even think about what happened . . . and we don't feel full or bloated after! We've heard that said of fermented pizza doughs, and with this crust, we really experience it.

225 grams warm water (110°F/45°C)

1½ teaspoons sugar

½ teaspoon active dry yeast

75 grams quinoa flour

50 grams potato starch

50 grams tapioca starch

12 grams coconut flour

1 teaspoon psyllium husk

1 teaspoon xanthan gum

¾ teaspoon salt

1 tablespoon olive oil, plus more for greasing

High-altitude modification: Increase the water to 250 grams.

1. In a small bowl, whisk together the water, sugar, and yeast. Set aside to allow the yeast to activate, about 5 minutes, until foamy.

2. In a medium bowl, whisk together the quinoa flour, potato starch, tapioca starch, coconut flour, psyllium husk, xanthan gum, and salt.

3. When the yeast mixture is foamy on top, add the oil and stir to combine.

4. Pour the yeast mixture into the flour mixture and stir vigorously with a spoon until it is smooth, thickens slightly, and forms a loose dough. It should be very sticky and too wet to hold.

5. Lightly grease a medium-sized container (glass or plastic).

6. Place the dough in the container and loosely cover. (If the container has a lid, place the lid squarely on top of the container but do *not* snap it tightly shut. This allows excess carbon dioxide from the fermentation to escape while preventing the dough from drying. Otherwise, covering the container with a plate or loosely with plastic wrap works well.)

7. Refrigerate for 48 hours.

8. At least 2 hours before you plan to make pizza, remove the container from the refrigerator to allow the dough to come to room temperature.

Pomodori Freschi

Apart from the crust itself—a delightful balance of char and chew—the small tomatoes that top this pizza are the star of the show. They're inspired by the datterini tomatoes popular in much of Italy, though flavorful grape or cherry tomatoes work just as well here.

Bench flour (page 10)

1 prepared Grilled Dough (pages 116 to 117)

1 tablespoon light olive oil, plus more for shaping and grilling the dough

5 ounces (140 g) fresh mozzarella

5 ounces (140 g) tricolor grape and/or cherry tomatoes, sliced into halves or quarters

10 basil leaves, chiffonade

Generous pinch coarse kosher salt

Extra virgin olive oil

1. **If using the quick dough,** set your oven rack in the middle position, place your baking steel on it, and preheat the oven to 550°F (285°C) for at least 1 hour; do not start step 3 until the *end* of the preheat. **If using the fermented dough,** complete steps 3 to 5 *before* preheating the oven and let rise for 45 minutes.

2. When the oven has been preheating for about 45 minutes, preheat your grill to 500°F (260°C) with the burners on high. Then clean and oil the grill grate.

3. **To shape the dough,** place a 15-inch (38 cm) square piece of parchment paper on a flat surface. Dust about 1 tablespoon bench flour onto the parchment.

4. Use a spatula to scrape the dough from the bowl onto the center of the parchment.

5. Generously oil your hands and press the dough into a 12- to 13-inch (30 x 33 cm) flat circle with no raised lip around the perimeter edge. If the dough

sticks at all, add more oil to your hands. The finished circle should be very thin (less than ¼ inch/6 mm thick) and smooth all the way to the edge (see page 19 for technique tips).

6. **To par-bake the crust,** use a lightly floured pizza peel to launch the dough-on-parchment onto the baking steel in the oven. Cook for 3 minutes.

7. Slide your pizza peel under the dough-on-parchment, remove from the oven, and transfer to your kitchen counter.

8. Lightly dust the pizza peel with more flour, especially along the leading edge of the peel, then slide the peel between the parchment and the crust so that the crust is directly on the peel.

9. **To finish the pizza,** turn the grill burners down to medium-low. (If using a charcoal grill, knock down the central fire and move most of the red hot coals toward the perimeter, so the pizza gets

> **Note:** Once the crust is par-baked, the rest of this recipe takes place on the grill. Stage all of your ingredients grill-side so you can stay there as you work through the recipe. Keep your grill covered whenever you're not working with the pizza to retain as much heat as possible.

both direct heat from beneath and indirect heat from around the sides.)

10. Brush the top of the crust with light olive oil from edge to edge, so that the pizza glistens but does not have any pools of oil.

11. Flop the pizza crust, top side down, onto the center of your grill. Grill for 45 seconds. Using tongs, rotate the crust 90 degrees and grill for 45 seconds more.

12. Using tongs, flip the pizza right-side up onto the center of the grill. Top with hand-torn pieces of the mozzarella and the tomatoes.

13. Close the lid and cook for 2 minutes. Rotate the pizza 90 degrees and grill for 2 minutes more, until the bottom of the pizza has well-defined grill marks and the mozzarella is evenly melted. If you would like to melt the cheese a little more, keep the burner directly under the pizza at medium-low, increase the side burners to high, and cook for 2 more minutes.

14. Using your pizza peel, transfer the pizza to a large cutting board. Sprinkle the basil and the salt evenly over the pizza. Then drizzle lightly with extra virgin olive oil. Let set for 2 minutes, then slice and serve hot.

Steak, Bacon, and Blue Cheese

☙ MAKES ONE 12- TO 13-INCH (30 X 33 CM) PIZZA ❧

This recipe is like a visit to your favorite steakhouse, but on a pizza.

8 ounces (225 g)
  beef sirloin steak

¼ teaspoon salt

1 teaspoon olive oil,
  plus more for shaping
  and grilling the
  dough

4 slices bacon, cut
  into pieces

Bench flour (page 10)

1 prepared Grilled
  Dough (pages 116
  to 117)

6 ounces (170 g)
  crumbled blue cheese
  (double-check
  gluten-free status)

1. If using the quick dough, set your oven rack in the middle position, place your baking steel on it, and preheat the oven to 550°F (285°C) for at least 1 hour; do not start step 5 until the *end* of the preheat. **If using the fermented dough,** complete steps 5 to 7 *before* preheating the oven and let rise for 45 minutes.

2. When the oven has been preheating for about 30 minutes, preheat your grill with the burners on high to 500°F (260°C). Then clean and oil the grill grate.

3. Season each side of the steak with the salt and grill until medium rare, about 5 minutes per side. Remove from the grill and rest for 10 minutes, then cut into thin slices across the grain. If necessary, re-clean and oil the grill grate.

4. Heat the oil in a sauté pan over medium-high heat and add the bacon. Cook until crispy, then remove from the heat. When the bacon is cool enough, crumble and set aside.

5. To shape the dough, place a 15-inch (38 cm) square piece of parchment paper on a flat surface. Dust about 1 tablespoon bench flour onto the parchment.

6. Use a spatula to scrape the dough from the bowl onto the center of the parchment.

7. Generously oil your hands and press the dough into a 12- to 13-inch (30 x 33 cm) flat circle, with no raised lip around the perimeter edge. If the dough sticks at all, add more oil to your hands. The finished circle should be very thin (less than ¼ inch/6 mm thick) and smooth all the way to the edge (see page 19 for technique tips).

8. To par-bake the crust, use a lightly floured pizza peel to launch the dough-on-parchment onto the baking steel in the oven. Cook for 3 minutes.

9. Slide your pizza peel under the dough-on-parchment, remove from the oven, and transfer to your kitchen counter.

10. Lightly dust the pizza peel with more flour, especially along the leading edge of the peel, then slide the peel between the parchment and the crust so that just the crust is directly on the peel.

11. To finish the pizza, turn the grill burners down to medium-low. (If using a charcoal grill, knock down the central fire and move most of the red hot coals toward the perimeter so the pizza gets both direct heat from beneath and indirect heat from around the sides.)

12. Brush the top of the crust with oil from edge to edge so the pizza glistens but does not have any pools of oil.

13. Flop the pizza crust, top side down, onto the center of your grill. Grill for 45 seconds. Using tongs, rotate the crust 90 degrees and grill for 45 seconds more.

14. Using tongs, flip the pizza right-side up onto the center of the grill. Top with blue cheese, bacon, and steak.

15. Close the lid and cook for 2 minutes. Rotate the pizza 90 degrees and grill for 2 minutes more, until the bottom of the pizza has well-defined grill marks.

CALIFORNIA-STYLE PIZZAS

With a dose of nutrient-rich teff in the dough and eclectic, farmers market–fresh toppings, these pizzas remind us of the best California has to offer. The dough itself is closest to our New York–style pizzas, so feel free to substitute any of those toppings on these California pizzas.

California Dough

Quick Version

◦⟋ MAKES ONE 12- TO 13-INCH (30 X 33 CM) PIZZA ⟍◦

The quick version of our California dough is a time saver that still delivers delicious pizza.

157 grams warm water (110°F/45°C)

1½ teaspoons sugar

1 teaspoon active dry yeast

50 grams brown rice flour

50 grams cornstarch

50 grams tapioca starch

12 grams teff flour

1 teaspoon ground psyllium husk

¾ teaspoon salt

¼ teaspoon xanthan gum

1 tablespoon olive oil

High-altitude modification: Increase the water to 175 grams.

1. In a small bowl, whisk together the water, sugar, and yeast. Set aside to allow the yeast to activate, about 5 minutes, until foamy.

2. In a medium bowl, whisk together the rice flour, cornstarch, tapioca starch, teff flour, psyllium husk, salt, and xanthan gum.

3. When the yeast mixture is foamy on top, add the oil and stir to combine.

4. Pour the yeast mixture into the flour mixture and stir vigorously with a spoon until it is smooth, there are no lumps, and it forms a wet dough.

California Dough

48-Hour Fermentation

≈ MAKES ONE 12- TO 13-INCH (30 X 33 CM) PIZZA ≈

This fermented dough is well worth the wait. Like the fermented New York–Style Dough, the edge of the crust develops an airier, chewier lip that springs back impressively.

157 grams warm water (110°F/45°C)

1½ teaspoons sugar

½ teaspoon active dry yeast

50 grams brown rice flour

50 grams cornstarch

50 grams tapioca starch

12 grams teff flour

1 teaspoon ground psyllium husk

¾ teaspoon salt

¼ teaspoon xanthan gum

1 tablespoon olive oil, plus more for greasing

High-altitude modification: Increase the water to 175 grams.

1. In a small bowl, whisk together the water, sugar, and yeast. Set aside to allow the yeast to activate, about 5 minutes, until foamy.

2. In a medium bowl, whisk together the rice flour, cornstarch, tapioca starch, teff flour, psyllium husk, salt, and xanthan gum.

3. When the yeast mixture is foamy on top, add the oil and stir to combine.

4. Pour the yeast mixture into the flour mixture and stir vigorously with a spoon until it is smooth, there are no lumps, and it forms a wet dough.

5. Lightly grease a medium-sized container (glass or plastic). Place the dough in the container and loosely cover. (If the container has a lid, place the lid squarely on top of the container but do *not* snap it tightly shut. This allows excess carbon dioxide from the fermentation to escape while preventing the dough from drying. Otherwise, covering the container with a plate or loosely with plastic wrap works well.)

6. Refrigerate for 48 hours.

7. At least 2 hours before you plan to make pizza, remove the container from the refrigerator to allow the dough to come to room temperature.

Barbecue Chicken

≈ MAKES ONE 12- TO 13-INCH (30 X 33 CM) PIZZA ≈

This pizza features our balanced barbecue sauce, which straddles the sweet-and-spicy divide, plus a finish of fresh cilantro. Using barbecue sauce both to coat the chicken and as the pizza sauce really packs it with amazing flavor. You can make the sauce while the oven is preheating.

1 cup (115 g) Shredded Chicken (page 173)

½ cup (115 g) plus 1 tablespoon Barbecue Sauce (page 173)

Bench flour (page 10)

1 prepared California Dough (pages 124 to 125)

Olive oil, for working the dough

6 ounces (170 g) shredded low-moisture mozzarella

¼ red onion, thinly sliced

1 carrot, julienned

1 tablespoon chopped fresh cilantro

1. If using the quick dough, set your oven rack in the middle position, place your baking steel on it, and preheat the oven to 550°F (285°C) for at least 1 hour; do not start step 3 until the *end* of the preheat. **If using the fermented dough,** complete steps 3 to 5 *before* preheating the oven and let rise for 1 hour.

2. While the oven is preheating, toss the Shredded Chicken in ¼ cup (55 g) of the Barbecue Sauce. Set aside.

3. To shape the dough, place a 15-inch (38 cm) square piece of parchment paper on a flat surface. Dust about 1 tablespoon bench flour onto the parchment.

4. Using a spatula, scrape the dough out of the bowl onto the center of the parchment.

5. With oiled hands, gently press the dough into a 12- to 13-inch (30 x 33 cm) circle, leaving a small lip of raised dough around the perimeter edge (see page 19 for technique tips).

6. To finish the pizza, spread ¼ cup (55 g) of the Barbecue Sauce over the surface of the crust. Top with mozzarella and then chicken, onion, and carrot.

7. Use a lightly floured pizza peel to launch the pizza-on-parchment onto the baking steel in the oven. Bake for 2 minutes.

8. Strip the parchment (page 22). Bake for 5 to 6 minutes with the pizza directly on the steel.

9. Remove the pizza from the oven and transfer to a large cutting board. Drizzle with the remaining tablespoon of Barbecue Sauce and garnish with the cilantro. Let set for 2 minutes, then slice and serve hot.

Thai Chicken

⊱ MAKES ONE 12- TO 13-INCH (30 X 33 CM) PIZZA ⊰

This recipe is chicken pad thai embodied on a pizza. It's inspired by a certain famous California-born pizza chain, but we've given it our own flare.

1 tablespoon olive oil, plus more for working the dough

One 1-inch (2.5 cm) piece fresh ginger, peeled and minced

1 garlic clove, minced

1 boneless skinless chicken breast, diced small

2 tablespoons peanut butter

2 tablespoons rice vinegar

2 tablespoons gluten-free soy sauce (such as wheat-free tamari)

2 tablespoons water

1 tablespoon packed brown sugar

Bench flour (page 10)

1 prepared California Dough (pages 124 to 125)

6 ounces (170 g) shredded low-moisture mozzarella

1 small carrot, grated

1 green onion, thinly sliced

¼ cup (30 g) bean sprouts, optional*

2 tablespoons chopped fresh cilantro

1. If using the quick dough, set your oven rack in the middle position, place your baking steel on it, and preheat the oven to 550°F (285°C) for at least 1 hour; do not start step 4 until the *end* of the preheat. **If using the fermented dough,** complete steps 4 to 6 *before* preheating the oven and let rise for 1 hour.

2. While the oven is preheating, heat the oil in a large sauté pan over medium-high heat. Add the ginger and garlic and sauté until fragrant, about 1 minute. Add the chicken and sauté until cooked through, about 5 minutes.

3. In a small bowl, whisk together the peanut butter, rice vinegar, soy sauce, water, and sugar. Add to the pan with the cooked chicken, decrease the heat to low, and cook until the sauce is slightly thickened, about 3 minutes.

4. To shape the dough, place a 15-inch (38 cm) square piece of parchment paper on a flat surface. Dust about 1 tablespoon bench flour onto the parchment.

5. Using a spatula, scrape the dough out of the bowl onto the center of the parchment.

6. With oiled hands, gently press the dough into a 12- to 13-inch (30 x 33 cm) circle, leaving a small lip of raised dough around the perimeter edge (see page 19 for technique tips).

7. To finish the pizza, spread the chicken and peanut sauce over the surface of the crust. Top with the mozzarella, then the carrot and green onion.

8. Use a lightly floured pizza peel to launch the pizza-on-parchment onto the baking steel in the oven. Bake for 2 minutes.

9. Strip the parchment (page 22). Bake for 5 to 6 minutes with the pizza directly on the steel.

10. Remove the pizza from the oven and transfer to a large cutting board. Top with the bean sprouts, if using, and cilantro. Let set for 2 minutes, then slice and serve hot.

* The US Department of Health and Human Services recommends that children, the elderly, and people with weak immune systems avoid raw sprouts because they can carry harmful bacteria.

Goat Cheese, Roasted Red Pepper, and Caramelized Onion

⌘ MAKES ONE 12- TO 13-INCH (30 X 33 CM) PIZZA ⌘

This makes a great pizza for a light lunch or an al fresco dinner on a summer's evening.

1 tablespoon olive oil, plus more for working the dough

½ sweet onion, sliced

2 ounces (55 g) cremini mushrooms, sliced

Bench flour (page 10)

1 prepared California Dough (pages 124 to 125)

¼ cup (60 g) drained, sliced roasted red peppers

3 ounces (85 g) goat cheese, crumbled

1 handful baby arugula

2 tablespoons Balsamic Glaze (page 132)

1. If using the quick dough, set your oven rack in the middle position, place your baking steel on it, and preheat the oven to 550°F (285°C) for at least 1 hour; do not start step 4 until the *end* of the preheat. **If using the fermented dough,** complete steps 4 to 6 *before* preheating the oven and let rise for 1 hour.

2. While the oven is preheating, heat the oil in a small sauté pan over medium heat. Add the onions and sauté until they are very soft and begin to caramelize, about 10 minutes. Remove from the pan and set aside.

3. Add the mushrooms along with a little extra oil, if needed. Cook until all of the water has released and evaporated, about 5 minutes. Remove the pan from the heat.

4. To shape the dough, place a 15-inch (38 cm) square piece of parchment paper on a flat surface. Dust about 1 tablespoon bench flour onto the parchment.

5. Using a spatula, scrape the dough out of the bowl onto the center of the parchment.

6. With oiled hands, gently press the dough into a 12- to 13-inch (30 x 33 cm) circle, leaving a small lip of raised dough around the perimeter edge (see page 19 for technique tips).

7. To finish the pizza, spread the onion, mushroom, red pepper, and goat cheese on the crust.

8. Use a lightly floured pizza peel to launch the pizza-on-parchment onto the baking steel in the oven. Bake for 2 minutes.

9. Strip the parchment (page 22). Bake for 5 to 6 minutes with the pizza directly on the steel.

10. Remove the pizza from the oven and transfer to a large cutting board. Top with arugula, then drizzle with the Balsamic Glaze. Let set for 2 minutes, then slice and serve hot.

Balsamic Glaze

MAKES 1/3 CUP (80 ML)

1 cup (240 ml) balsamic vinegar

1 tablespoon maple syrup

Heat the vinegar and maple syrup in a small saucepan over high heat and bring to a boil. Reduce the heat to medium and simmer for 10 to 15 minutes, until the mixture has reduced by $2/3$ and coats the back of a spoon. Use immediately or store in a sealed container in the refrigerator for up to 2 weeks.

Eggplant and Sun-Dried Tomato

⊙ MAKES ONE 12- TO 13-INCH (30 X 33 CM) PIZZA ⊙

Eggplant is a hugely underrated pizza topping. When roasted, it becomes soft and creamy yet richly flavorful. This recipe gives it some time in the spotlight.

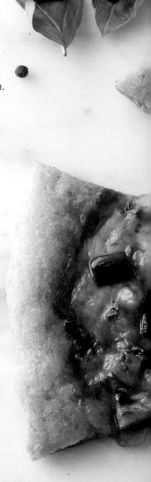

2 tablespoons olive oil, plus more for working the dough

1 Japanese eggplant, ½-inch (13 mm) diced (or half of a purple eggplant, peeled and diced)

⅛ teaspoon salt

⅛ teaspoon ground black pepper

Bench flour (page 10)

1 prepared California Dough (pages 124 to 125)

½ cup (115 g) puréed canned San Marzano tomatoes

3 ounces (85 g) shredded low-moisture mozzarella

3 ounces (85 g) shredded provolone

¼ cup (55 g) drained, sliced sun-dried tomatoes

8 fresh basil leaves

1. If using the quick dough, set your oven rack in the middle position, place your baking steel on it, and preheat the oven to 550°F (285°C) for at least 1 hour; do not start step 3 until the *end* of the preheat. **If using the fermented dough,** complete steps 3 to 5 *before* preheating the oven and let rise for 1 hour.

2. While the oven is preheating, toss the oil and eggplant, season with salt and pepper, and place on a baking sheet. Roast in the preheating oven for 10 minutes to soften. Remove from the oven and set aside.

3. To shape the dough, place a 15-inch (38 cm) square piece of parchment paper on a flat surface. Dust about 1 tablespoon bench flour onto the parchment.

4. Using a spatula, scrape the dough out of the bowl onto the center of the parchment.

5. With oiled hands, gently press the dough into a 12- to 13-inch (30 x 33 cm) circle, leaving a small lip of raised dough around the perimeter edge (see page 19 for technique tips).

6. To finish the pizza, spread the puréed tomatoes over the surface of the crust. Sprinkle on the cheeses, sun-dried tomatoes, and eggplant.

7. Use a lightly floured pizza peel to launch the pizza-on-parchment onto the baking steel in the oven. Bake for 2 minutes.

8. Strip the parchment (page 22). Bake for 5 to 6 minutes with the pizza directly on the steel.

9. Remove the pizza from the oven and transfer to a large cutting board. Top with the basil. Let set for 2 minutes, then slice and serve hot.

GRAIN-FREE PIZZAS

Most of the pizzas in this cookbook use flour blends that combine high-protein, gluten-free grain flours with starches. In this chapter, you'll find pizza styles—and crusts—that are gloriously grain-free.

From naturally grain-free, gluten-free farinata, which is made from chickpeas, to the popular cauliflower crust, to even a zucchini crust, if you're looking for an alternative base with no grains, this chapter is for you.

Cinque Terre Farinata
[Rosemary, Shallot, Zucchini]

⤳ MAKES ONE 10-INCH (25 CM) PIE ⤳

This is the flavor combo that launched our love affair with farinata. It's great any time of year but especially in summer when young, fresh zucchini are in season.

180 grams chickpea (garbanzo bean) flour

472 grams warm water (110°F/45°C)

1 tablespoon chopped fresh rosemary

1 teaspoon salt

5 tablespoons olive oil

1 shallot, thinly sliced

1 small, slender zucchini, thinly sliced into coins

Note: Soak the chickpea flour and water ahead of time so it's ready when time to bake the farinata.

1. In a medium bowl, whisk together the chickpea flour and water and let sit uncovered at room temperature on the kitchen counter for at least 3 hours and up to 8 hours.

2. Place a 10-inch (25 cm) cast-iron skillet (or other heavy, oven-safe skillet) in the oven and preheat the oven to 500°F (260°C). Once the oven has finished preheating, leave the skillet in for 30 minutes to allow it to also come up to temperature.

3. While the oven is preheating, skim off and discard any foam that has formed on the surface of the chickpea mixture. Add the rosemary, salt, and 2 tablespoons of the oil and stir to combine.

4. Heat ½ tablespoon of the oil in a small sauté pan over medium-high heat and sauté the shallot until soft but not caramelized. Set aside.

5. Toss the sliced zucchini in ½ tablespoon of the oil.

6. With well-insulated oven mitts, carefully remove the skillet from the oven and place on a heat-safe surface. Add the remaining 2 tablespoons of the oil to the skillet and swirl to coat the bottom. (Leave an oven mitt or dry kitchen towel draped over the handle of the skillet so you don't accidentally grab the scorching-hot pan with your bare hands.)

7. Pour the batter away from you into the skillet. After the wet dough has settled, arrange the shallot over the surface of the farinata, then add the zucchini.

8. Place the entire skillet back into the oven and bake for 25 minutes, or until the edges are deeply browned and slightly crispy.

9. Remove the skillet from the oven and transfer the farinata onto a cutting board. (To easily remove the farinata from the pan, coax a metal spatula under one edge of the crust, then tilt the skillet to slide the farinata onto the cutting board.) Serve warm or at room temperature.

Pesto Farinata

We think of farinata as pizza's cousin. The crust is made from chickpea flour and naturally gluten-free. Farinata originated in Genoa, Italy, but its popularity has spread throughout Liguria and beyond. We first discovered great farinata on a 2013 trip to Italy's Cinque Terre, and it's been a part of our dinner menu ever since.

180 grams chickpea (garbanzo bean) flour

472 grams warm water (110°F/45°C)

1 teaspoon salt

4 tablespoons olive oil

1 heirloom tomato, thinly sliced

¼ cup (80 g) Pesto (page 61)

High-altitude modification: not required.

Note: Soak the chickpea flour and water ahead of time so it's ready when time to bake the farinata.

1. In a medium bowl, whisk together the chickpea flour and water and let sit uncovered at room temperature on the kitchen counter for at least 3 hours and up to 8 hours.

2. Place a 10-inch (25 cm) cast-iron skillet (or other heavy, oven-safe skillet) in the oven and preheat the oven to 500°F (260°C). Once the oven has finished preheating, leave the skillet in for 30 minutes to allow it to also come up to temperature.

3. **While the oven is preheating,** skim off and discard any foam that has formed on the surface of the chickpea mixture. Add the salt and 2 tablespoons of the oil and stir to combine.

4. With well-insulated oven mitts, carefully remove the skillet from the oven and place on a heat-safe surface. Add the remaining 2 tablespoons oil to the skillet and swirl to coat the bottom. (Leave an oven mitt or dry kitchen towel draped over the handle of the skillet so you don't accidentally grab the scorching-hot pan with your bare hands.)

5. Pour the batter away from you into the skillet. After the wet dough has settled, arrange the tomato slices on the surface of the farinata.

6. Place the skillet back into the oven and bake for 25 minutes, or until the edges of the dough are deeply browned and slightly crispy.

7. Remove the skillet from the oven and transfer the farinata onto a cutting board. (To easily remove the farinata from the pan, coax a metal spatula under one edge of the crust, then tilt the skillet to slide the farinata onto the cutting board.)

8. With a spoon, drizzle the Pesto over the farinata. If desired, use an offset spatula to spread it evenly over the surface. Serve warm or at room temperature.

Cauliflower Crust

This cauliflower crust does what many others don't: It stays firm enough that you can actually hold a slice in your hand, unlike floppy recipes we've come across on the internet. But perhaps most impressively, this crust has found favor among our children's friends—a true testament!

2 pounds (910 g/ 1 large head) cauliflower florets

1 egg

2 ounces (55 g) shredded low-moisture mozzarella

1 teaspoon dried basil

1 teaspoon dried oregano

1 teaspoon garlic powder

¼ teaspoon salt

¼ teaspoon ground black pepper

High-altitude modification: not required.

Note: As an alternative to fresh cauliflower, you can buy frozen riced cauliflower. If doing so, defrost the cauliflower and skip step 2.

1. Set your oven rack in the middle position and place your baking steel on it. Preheat the oven to 400°F (205°C) for at least 30 minutes.

2. Boil or steam the cauliflower florets until tender, about 10 minutes. Drain and allow to cool. Place the florets in the food processor in batches and pulse until they look like quinoa, scraping down the sides periodically.

3. Scrape all of the cauliflower into a kitchen towel and squeeze out as much liquid as possible.

4. Place the cauliflower in a bowl and add the remaining ingredients. Stir to combine.

5. Place a 15-inch (38 cm) square piece of parchment on the counter and press the cauliflower mixture with your hands into a 12-inch (30 cm) circle. It should be thin.

6. Use your pizza peel to launch the crust-on-parchment onto the steel and bake for 30 minutes.

7. Remove the crust-on-parchment from the oven and flip the crust over on the parchment paper. Return it to the oven and bake for 5 minutes with the top side down.

8. Remove the crust from the oven and flip it onto a new piece of parchment paper, returning the top side up.

Zucchini Crust

ᗌ MAKES ONE 12-INCH (30 CM) PIZZA ᗌ

Move over, cauliflower. It's time to share the pizza stage with another grain-free, veggie-based crust: zucchini.

1½ pounds
  (680 g/3½ cups)
  coarsely grated
  zucchini

1 teaspoon salt

2 eggs

28 grams almond flour

20 grams tapioca
  starch

2 ounces (55 g)
  shredded low-
  moisture mozzarella

2 tablespoons grated
  Parmesan

1 teaspoon dried basil

1 teaspoon dried
  oregano

½ teaspoon ground
  black pepper

*High-altitude
modification: not
required.*

1. Set your oven rack in the middle position and place your baking steel on it. Preheat the oven to 400°F (205°C) for at least 30 minutes.

2. Place the zucchini in a large bowl and sprinkle with the salt. Allow to set for 15 minutes. Then scrape into a kitchen towel and squeeze out as much liquid as possible.

3. Return the zucchini to the bowl and add the remaining ingredients. Stir to combine.

4. Place a 15-inch (38 cm) square piece of parchment on the counter and press the zucchini mixture into a 12-inch (30 cm) circle. It should be thin.

5. Use your pizza peel to launch the crust-on-parchment onto the steel and bake for 30 minutes.

6. Remove the crust-on-parchment from the oven and flip the crust over on the parchment paper. Return it to the oven and bake for 5 minutes with the top side down.

7. Remove the crust from the oven and flip it onto a new piece of parchment paper, returning the top side up.

Brussels Sprouts and Bacon

⚬ MAKES ONE 12-INCH (30 CM) PIZZA ⚬

Make this pizza in late summer or early fall when brussels sprouts are in season. The salty bacon really brings out their flavor. Parcooking the brussels sprouts ensures that they finish cooking perfectly atop the pizza.

4 slices bacon

½ small sweet onion, thinly sliced

¼ teaspoon plus ⅛ teaspoon salt

8 ounces (225 g) small brussels sprouts, quartered

5 ounces (140 g) shredded low-moisture mozzarella

1 prepared Cauliflower Crust (page 141) or Zucchini Crust (page 142)

1. Set your oven rack in the middle position and place your baking steel on it. Preheat the oven to 400°F (205°C) for at least 30 minutes.

2. While the oven is preheating, heat a heavy sauté pan over medium-high heat. Cook the bacon until it is crispy, then remove from the pan and set aside.

3. Remove all but 1 tablespoon of the bacon fat and set aside. Sauté the onion and ⅛ teaspoon salt until the onions are soft and begin to caramelize, about 5 minutes. Remove from the pan and set aside.

4. Add the brussels sprouts and the remaining ¼ teaspoon salt to the pan and sauté until soft and beginning to char, about 10 minutes. Add the reserved bacon fat to the pan if needed. Remove from the heat and set aside.

5. Switch the oven to broil.

6. To finish the pizza, sprinkle the mozzarella over the surface of the crust, leaving a ¼-inch (6 mm) border. Add the onion and brussels sprouts, then crumble the bacon on top.

7. Slide the pizza back into the oven, stripping the parchment (page 22) so the crust is directly on the steel. Leave the pizza under the broiler until the cheese is melted, about 5 minutes.

8. Remove the pizza from the oven and let cool for 5 minutes, then slice and serve hot.

Primavera and Ricotta

Although best in late spring and early summer, this veggie-packed pizza can be enjoyed year-round.

1 small red onion, thinly sliced

½ small red bell pepper, thinly sliced

1 small zucchini, thinly sliced

4 cremini mushrooms, thinly sliced

2 tablespoons olive oil

1 teaspoon herbes de Provence

⅛ teaspoon salt

⅛ teaspoon ground black pepper

½ cup (125 g) Marinara Sauce (page 155)

1 prepared Cauliflower Crust (page 141) or Zucchini Crust (page 142)

4 ounces (115 g) shredded low-moisture mozzarella

¼ cup (55 g) Ricotta (page 202)

1. Set your oven rack in the middle position with the baking steel on it and preheat to 400°F (205°C).

2. Toss the vegetables with the oil, herbes de Provence, salt, and pepper on a baking sheet. Spread in a single layer and bake for 15 minutes, or until the vegetables soften slightly and begin to turn golden brown.

3. Remove the vegetables from the oven. Switch the oven to broil.

4. Spread the Marinara Sauce on top of the crust, leaving about a ¼-inch (6 mm) border. Sprinkle the mozzarella over the sauce, then the vegetables. Dollop with the Ricotta.

5. Slide the pizza back into the oven, stripping the parchment (page 22) so the crust is directly on the steel. Leave the pizza under the broiler until the cheese is melted, about 5 minutes.

6. Remove the pizza from the oven and let cool for 5 minutes, then slice and serve hot.

Mediterranean

Olive tapenade. Artichokes. Sun-dried tomatoes. Feta cheese. This pizza is the next best thing to a sailboat cruise island-hopping through the Greek isles!

½ cup (200 g) Olive Tapenade (see below)

1 prepared Cauliflower Crust (page 141) or Zucchini Crust (page 142)

4 ounces (115 g) marinated artichoke hearts, quartered

¼ cup (55 g) drained sliced sun-dried tomatoes

2 ounces (55 g) feta, crumbled

1. Set your oven rack in the middle position and place your baking steel on it. Preheat the oven to 400°F (205°C) for at least 30 minutes. Then switch the oven to broil.

2. Spread the Olive Tapenade over the crust, leaving a ¼-inch (6 mm) border. Add the artichoke hearts, sun-dried tomatoes, and the feta.

3. Slide the pizza back into the oven, stripping the parchment (page 22) so the crust is directly on the steel. Leave the pizza under the broiler until the cheese is melted, about 5 minutes.

4. Remove the pizza from the oven and let cool for 5 minutes, then slice and serve hot.

Olive Tapenade

MAKES ½ CUP (200 G)

½ cup (85 g) brined pitted olives (e.g., Nicoise, kalamata)

1 garlic clove

2 tablespoons olive oil

1 tablespoon lemon juice

2 teaspoons capers

2 teaspoons packed chopped fresh parsley

2 teaspoons packed chopped fresh basil

¼ teaspoon anchovy paste

¼ teaspoon dried oregano

Combine all of the ingredients in a blender. Blend until finely chopped, stopping periodically to scrape down the side. Use immediately or store in refrigerator.

FRIED AND FILLED

The Campania region in and around Naples, Italy, is known for its fried foods and its enormous calzones. Thanks to the Italian diaspora around the turn of the twentieth century, these close relatives of classic pizza have gone global, too. In this chapter, we offer up several gluten-free options, ranging from a fried montanara pizza crust to oven-baked calzones and handheld pizza pockets.

Montanara Dough

The montanara pizza is a classic Neapolitan version of pizza fritta: fried pizza. The deep-fried dough turns a rich golden brown yet amazingly doesn't get greasy. It knocked our socks off when we tried pizzaiolo Angelo Caprio's version at Pizzeria Mascagni in Naples, Italy.

80 grams warm water (110°F/45°C)

1 teaspoon sugar

1 teaspoon active dry yeast

20 grams potato starch

20 grams tapioca starch

20 grams millet flour

20 grams quinoa flour

10 grams brown rice flour

½ teaspoon ground psyllium husk

½ teaspoon salt

½ teaspoon xanthan gum

2 tablespoons olive oil

High-altitude modification: not required.

1. In a small bowl, whisk together the water, sugar, and yeast. Set aside to allow the yeast to activate, about 5 minutes, until foamy.

2. In a medium bowl, whisk together the potato starch, tapioca starch, millet flour, quinoa flour, rice flour, psyllium husk, salt, and xanthan gum.

3. When the yeast mixture is foamy on top, add the oil and stir to combine.

4. Pour the yeast mixture into the flour mixture and stir vigorously with a spoon until it is smooth, there are no lumps, and it forms a loose dough.

Marinara Montanara

A hearty marinara sauce is a traditional topping for montanara pizza. This marinara recipe is inspired by the gluten-free marinara pizza at legendary Pizzeria Starita a Materdei in Naples. The pizzeria has been around since 1901, and during our visit in 2018, we were privileged to meet pizzaiolo Don Antonio himself.

1 quart (1 L) frying oil (such as vegetable, peanut, or canola)

Bench flour (page 10)

1 prepared Montanara Dough (page 152)

Superfine rice flour, for working the dough

⅔ cup (165 g) Marinara Sauce (page 155), heated through

2 tablespoons grated Parmesan

2 tablespoons Ricotta (page 202)

5 basil leaves

1. Heat the oil in a 10-inch (25 cm) heavy sauté pan (or cast-iron skillet) over medium-high heat, until the oil reaches 375°F (190°C).

2. To shape the dough, place a 15-inch (38 cm) square piece of parchment paper on a flat surface. Dust about 2 teaspoons bench flour onto the parchment.

3. Using a spatula, scrape the dough out of the bowl onto the center of the parchment and smooth the dough.

4. Coat your hands with superfine rice flour and sprinkle additional flour over the dough. Carefully tease the dough into a flat

9-inch (23 cm) circle, sprinkling just enough additional flour to prevent the dough from sticking to your hands (see page 20 for technique tips).

5. To finish the pizza, flip the dough off the parchment onto your hand and gently slide it into the hot oil. Cook the crust for 1 minute on the first side, then carefully flip the dough without splashing the oil and cook on the second side for 1 to 1½ minutes, until golden brown.

6. Use tongs to transfer the crust onto a paper towel. Transfer to a plate and spoon on the Marinara Sauce, sprinkle with the Parmesan, and dollop on the Ricotta. Finish with basil leaves, then slice and serve hot.

Marinara Sauce

MAKES 2½ CUPS (625 G)

2 tablespoons olive oil

6 garlic cloves, minced

½ medium yellow onion, diced

2 cups (455 g) puréed canned San Marzano tomatoes

10 grape tomatoes, quartered

1 tablespoon tomato paste

1 teaspoon dried basil

1 teaspoon dried oregano

1 teaspoon sugar

¼ teaspoon salt

⅛ teaspoon red pepper flakes

1. Heat the oil in a large sauté pan over medium-high heat. Add the garlic and onion and sauté until fragrant and the onions start to soften, about 3 minutes.

2. Add the remaining ingredients and simmer over medium-low heat for about 10 minutes, stirring occasionally, until the sauce has thickened and is no longer watery. Use immediately or store in refrigerator.

Garlic Montanara

In this simple fried pizza, the crust is the star of the show. Garlic lovers will also rejoice!

1 quart (1 L) frying oil (e.g., vegetable, peanut, canola)

2 tablespoons extra virgin olive oil

4 garlic cloves, minced

Bench flour (page 10)

1 prepared Montanara Dough (page 152)

Superfine rice flour, for working the dough

2 tablespoons grated Pecorino Romano

1 tablespoon chopped fresh parsley

1. Heat the frying oil in a 10-inch (25 cm) heavy sauté pan (or cast-iron skillet) over medium-high heat, until the oil reaches 375°F (190°C).

2. Combine the olive oil and garlic in a small bowl. Set aside.

3. To shape the dough, place a 15-inch (38 cm) square piece of parchment paper on a flat surface. Dust about 2 teaspoons bench flour onto the parchment.

4. Using a spatula, scrape the dough out of the bowl onto the center of the parchment and smooth the surface of the dough.

5. Coat your fingers and hands with superfine rice flour and sprinkle additional flour over the dough. Carefully tease the dough into a flat 9-inch (23 cm) circle, sprinkling just enough additional flour to prevent the dough from sticking to your hands (see page 20 for technique tips).

6. To finish the pizza, flip the dough off the parchment onto your hand and gently slide it into the hot oil. Cook the crust for 1 minute on the first side, then carefully flip the dough without splashing the oil and cook on the second side for 1 to 1½ minutes, until golden brown.

7. Use tongs to transfer the crust onto a paper towel. Transfer to a plate and drizzle the garlic olive oil over the crust, then sprinkle with the Pecorino Romano. Garnish with the chopped parsley, then slice and serve hot.

Sausage and Pepperoni Calzone

⌒ MAKES ONE 11-INCH (28 CM) CALZONE ⌒

When it comes to self-contained, handheld meals, few foods are better than a calzone. This recipe leverages our New York–Style Dough but adopts special techniques so you can handle the soft dough and form a beautifully sealed pocket.

1 teaspoon olive oil, plus more for working the dough and finishing the calzone

5 ounces (140 g) mild Italian sausage, removed from casings

1 ounce (30 g) small "coin" pepperoni

Bench flour (page 10)

1 prepared New York–Style Dough (Quick Version, page 32)

4 ounces (115 g) shredded low-moisture mozzarella

½ cup (115 g) New York–Style Tomato Sauce (page 35), optional

High-altitude modification: not required

1. Set your oven rack in the middle position and place your baking steel on it. Preheat the oven to 550°F (285°C) for at least 1 hour.

2. While the oven is preheating, heat the oil in a small sauté pan over medium-high heat. Cook the sausage until lightly brown, about 5 minutes. Remove from the pan, add the pepperoni, and cook for 1 minute to sweat out the oil. Remove the pan from the heat and set aside.

3. To shape the dough, place a 15-inch (38 cm) square piece of parchment paper on a flat surface. Dust about 1 tablespoon bench flour onto the parchment.

4. Using a spatula, scrape the dough out of the bowl onto the center of the parchment.

5. With oiled hands, gently press the dough into a flat 11-inch (28 cm) circle (see page 19 for technique tips).

6. To finish the calzone, spread half of the mozzarella over one half of the dough, leaving a ½-inch (13 mm) border. Place the sausage and pepperoni on the mozzarella. Top with the remaining mozzarella.

7. Slide your hand under the parchment and in one smooth motion fold the untopped side of the dough over the half with the fillings. Flip the dough so that the edges of the calzone line up well. Press the edges together with oiled fingers so the calzone is well sealed. Leave the parchment paper stuck to the top of the calzone.

8. Use the pizza peel to slide the entire calzone in its parchment wrapper onto the baking steel. Bake for 5 minutes.

9. Remove the calzone from the oven and slide it onto a baking sheet. Remove the parchment. Return the pan with the calzone on it to the oven, placing it directly onto the baking steel. Bake for 7 minutes.

10. Remove the calzone from the oven and switch the oven to broil. Mist or brush the surface of the calzone with oil just until it glistens. Return to the oven under the broiler for 1 minute, or until the surface is golden.

11. Remove the calzone from the oven and let set for 2 minutes. Slice and serve hot with the Tomato Sauce on the side (optional).

Ham and Ricotta Calzone

Ò Peperino e Milano is a Neapolitan-style pizzeria in the heart of Milan, Italy. Their dedicated gluten-free kitchen offers an impressive array of fried options, including one of the largest calzones we've ever seen. This recipe, filled with the popular duo of ham and ricotta, is in their honor.

Bench flour (page 10)

1 prepared New York–Style Dough (Quick Version, page 32)

Olive oil, for working the dough and finishing the calzone

4 ounces (115 g) shredded low-moisture mozzarella

4 ounces (115 g) thinly sliced deli ham

½ cup (115 g) Ricotta (page 202)

½ cup (115 g) New York–Style Tomato Sauce (page 35), optional

High-altitude modification: not required

1. Set your oven rack in the middle position and place your baking steel on it. Preheat the oven to 550°F (285°C) for at least 1 hour.

2. To shape the dough, place a 15-inch (38 cm) square piece of parchment paper on a flat surface. Dust about 1 tablespoon bench flour onto the parchment.

3. Using a spatula, scrape the dough out of the bowl onto the center of the parchment.

4. With oiled hands, gently press the dough into a flat 11-inch (28 cm) circle (see page 19 for technique tips).

5. To finish the calzone, spread half of the mozzarella over one half of the dough, leaving a ½-inch (13 mm) border. Place the ham and Ricotta on the mozzarella. Top with the remaining half of the mozzarella.

6. Slide your hand under the parchment and, in one smooth motion, fold the untopped side of the dough onto the half with the fillings. Flip the dough so that the edges of the calzone line up well.

Press the edges together with oiled fingers so the calzone is well sealed. Leave the parchment paper stuck to the top of the calzone.

7. Use the pizza peel to slide the calzone in its parchment wrapper onto the baking steel. Bake for 5 minutes.

8. Remove the calzone from the oven and slide it onto a baking sheet. Remove the parchment. Return the pan with the calzone to the oven, placing it directly onto the baking steel. Bake for 7 minutes.

9. Remove the calzone from the oven and switch the oven to broil. Mist or brush the surface of the calzone with oil just until it glistens. Broil for 1 minute, or until the surface is golden.

10. Remove the calzone from the oven and let set for 2 minutes. Slice and serve hot with the Tomato Sauce on the side (optional).

Pizza Pockets

MAKES THREE 3 X 7-INCH (7.5 X 18 CM) PIZZA POCKETS

When you need a personal-size snack on the go—or your family and friends can't agree on the fillings for a calzone to share—these pizza pockets are a great way to give each person what they want.

Bench flour (page 10)

1 prepared New York–Style Dough (Quick Version, page 32)

Olive oil, for working the dough and finishing the pockets

6 ounces (170 g) shredded low-moisture mozzarella

21 small "coin" pepperoni slices, 7 per pocket (1½ ounces/40 g)

4½ tablespoons New York–Style Tomato Sauce (page 35)

High-altitude modification: not required

1. Set your oven rack in the middle position and place your baking steel on it. Preheat the oven to 550°F (285°C) for at least 1 hour.

2. To shape the dough, cut three 8-inch (20 cm) squares of parchment. Dust each with bench flour.

3. Using a spatula, scrape the dough out of the bowl, dividing it evenly onto the three pieces of parchment.

4. With oiled hands, gently press each piece of dough into a flat 7-inch (18 cm) square (see page 19 for technique tips).

5. To finish the pockets, spread about 1 ounce (30 g/a generous pinch) mozzarella over one half of each dough, leaving a ½-inch (13 mm) border. Place 7 pepperoni slices in a shingled row on top of the mozzarella on each dough. Spread 1½ tablespoons of the Tomato Sauce on top of the pepperoni on each dough, then top each with 1 ounce (30 g) mozzarella.

6. Slide your hand under the parchment and, in one smooth motion, fold the untopped side of the dough onto the half with the fillings. Flip the dough so that the edges of the pockets line up well. Press the edges together with oiled fingers so

the pizza pockets are well sealed. Leave the parchment paper stuck to the top of the pockets.

7. Use the pizza peel to slide the pizza pockets in their parchment wrappers onto the baking steel. Bake for 4 minutes.

8. Remove the pizza pockets from the oven and slide them onto a baking sheet. Remove the parchment. Return the pan with the pockets on it to the oven, placing the pan directly onto the baking steel. Bake for 5 minutes.

9. Remove the pockets from the oven and switch the oven to broil. Mist or brush the surface of the pockets with oil just until it glistens. Broil for 1 minute, or until the surface is golden.

10. Remove the pockets from the oven and let set for 2 minutes. Serve hot.

FOCACCIA
AND
FLATBREAD
— PIZZAS —

From classic Italian focaccia to delightfully puffy flatbreads, this chapter is a refreshing departure from the red-sauce-and-mozzarella formula that dominates pizza making.

Rosemary Focaccia

⤳ MAKES ONE QUARTER-SHEET-PAN (9 X 13 INCHES/23 X 33 CM) ⤳

Focaccia is a versatile oven-baked Italian flatbread eaten for breakfast, as an antipasto before dinner, and whenever the craving strikes. This focaccia *al rosmarino* is a common classic, though you could substitute other herbs. Our gluten-free version has all the delightful sponginess of the original. Try dipping it in extra virgin olive oil seasoned with fresh-cracked black pepper and a splash of balsamic vinegar.

360 grams warm water (110°F/45°C)

1 tablespoon sugar

1 tablespoon plus 2 teaspoons active dry yeast (2 packets)

155 grams white rice flour

85 grams quinoa flour

75 grams tapioca starch

65 grams potato starch

1 tablespoon plus 1 teaspoon ground psyllium husk

1 tablespoon chopped fresh rosemary

1½ teaspoons salt

1 teaspoon garlic powder

5 tablespoons olive oil, plus more for pressing out the dough

Coarse kosher salt

High-altitude modification: increase the water to 400 grams and decrease the yeast to 1 tablespoon.

1. In a small bowl, whisk together the water, sugar, and yeast. Set aside to allow the yeast to activate, about 5 minutes, until foamy.

2. In a medium bowl, whisk together the rice flour, quinoa flour, tapioca starch, potato starch, psyllium husk, rosemary, salt, and garlic powder.

3. When the yeast mixture is foamy on top, add 3 tablespoons of the oil and stir to combine.

4. Add the yeast mixture to the flours and stir vigorously until completely smooth. If using an electric mixer, mix only until the dough is smooth. Do not overmix.

5. Oil a well-seasoned or nonstick dark quarter sheet pan with 1 tablespoon of the oil. Use a spatula to scrape the dough onto the pan and oil your hands to press the dough out evenly. Set in a warm place and cover with an inverted cake pan. (The dough will rise up to the lip of the pan. Make sure the inverted cake pan leaves enough headroom so it doesn't touch the risen dough.) Leave to rise for 2 hours.

6. Close to the end of the rise time, preheat the oven to 300°F (150°C).

7. Bake for 45 minutes.

8. Remove the focaccia from the oven and increase the oven temperature to 450°F (230°C).

9. Brush with the remaining tablespoon of oil, sprinkle lightly with kosher salt, and return to the oven for 10 minutes, or until the surface is golden brown.

10. Remove the focaccia from the oven, transfer to a wire rack, and let cool for 10 minutes. Then slice and serve warm or at room temperature.

Olive [or Tomato] Focaccia

⌒ MAKES ONE QUARTER-SHEET-PAN (9 X 13 INCHES/23 X 33 CM) ⌒

This focaccia is studded with your choice of olives or tomatoes, and was a huge hit at Kelli's book club. Try pairing it with a glass of your favorite Italian wine.

360 grams warm water (110°F/45°C)

1 tablespoon sugar

1 tablespoon plus 2 teaspoons active dry yeast (2 packets)

155 grams white rice flour

85 grams quinoa flour

75 grams tapioca starch

65 grams potato starch

1 tablespoon plus 1 teaspoon ground psyllium husk

1½ teaspoons salt

1 teaspoon garlic powder

1 teaspoon chopped rosemary

1 teaspoon dried basil

1 teaspoon dried oregano

5 tablespoons olive oil, plus more for pressing out the dough

½ cup (85 g) pitted Kalamata olives or grape tomatoes

⅛ teaspoon coarse kosher salt

High-altitude modification: increase the water to 400 grams and decrease the yeast to 1 tablespoon.

1. In a small bowl, whisk together the water, sugar, and yeast. Set aside to allow the yeast to activate, about 5 minutes, until foamy.

2. In a medium bowl, whisk together the rice flour, quinoa flour, tapioca starch, potato starch, psyllium husk, salt, garlic powder, rosemary, basil, and oregano.

3. When the yeast mixture is foamy on top, add 3 tablespoons of the oil and stir to combine.

4. Add the yeast mixture to the flours and stir vigorously until completely smooth. If using an electric mixer, mix only until the dough is smooth. Do not overmix.

5. Oil a well-seasoned or nonstick dark quarter sheet pan with 1 tablespoon of the oil. Use a spatula to scrape the dough into the pan and oil your hands to press the dough out evenly. Set in a warm place and cover with an inverted cake pan. (The dough will rise up to the lip of the pan. Make sure the inverted cake pan leaves enough headroom so it doesn't touch the risen dough.) Leave to rise for 2 hours.

6. Close to the end of the rise time, preheat the oven to 300°F (150°C).

7. At the end of the rise, press the olives or grape tomatoes into the dough. Bake for 45 minutes.

8. Remove the focaccia from the oven and increase the oven temperature to 450°F (230°C). Brush with the remaining tablespoon oil, sprinkle lightly with the kosher salt, and return to the oven for 10 minutes, or until the surface is golden brown.

9. Remove the focaccia from the oven, transfer to a wire rack, and let cool for 10 minutes. Then slice and serve warm or at room temperature.

Butternut Squash Flatbread

This flatbread bursts with autumn flavors, thanks to ingredients such as butternut squash and sage. Thanksgiving appetizer, anyone?

Bench flour (page 10)

1 prepared New York–Style Dough (Quick Version, page 32)

2 tablespoons olive oil, plus more for working the dough

6 ounces (170 g) butternut squash, peeled and diced into ¼-inch (6 mm) pieces (about 1 cup)

¼ teaspoon plus ⅛ teaspoon salt

1 tablespoon butter

¼ sweet onion, sliced

2 tablespoons chopped fresh sage

2 ounces (55 g) goat cheese, crumbled

1. Set your oven rack in the middle position and place your baking steel on it. Preheat the oven to 550°F (285°C) for at least 1 hour.

2. While the oven is preheating, shape the dough: Place a 15-inch (38 cm) square piece of parchment paper on a flat surface. Dust about 1 tablespoon bench flour onto the parchment.

3. Using a spatula, scrape the dough out of the bowl onto the center of the parchment.

4. Generously coat your hands with oil and gently press the dough into a uniformly thick 9 x 14-inch (23 x 36 cm) oval. Allow the dough to rise for 20 minutes.

5. While the dough is rising, toss the squash, 1 tablespoon of the oil, and ⅛ teaspoon salt together and spread in a single layer on a baking sheet. Roast in the preheating oven for 10 minutes, until the squash is soft and lightly browned. Remove from the oven and set aside.

6. Add the remaining tablespoon oil to a sauté pan with the butter and heat over medium heat. Add the onion and ¼ teaspoon salt and cook until the onion is soft and begins to caramelize.

7. Add the sage, cook for 1 minute, and remove from the heat. Add the squash and toss to combine. Set aside.

8. To finish the flatbread, distribute the squash mixture over the crust. Add the goat cheese.

9. Use a lightly floured pizza peel to launch the flatbread-on-parchment onto the baking steel in the oven. Bake for 2 minutes.

10. Strip the parchment (page 22). Bake for 6 to 7 minutes with the flatbread directly on the steel.

11. Remove the flatbread from the oven and transfer to a large cutting board. Let set for 2 minutes, then slice and serve hot.

Barbecue Chicken Flatbread

⌁ MAKES ONE 9 X 14-INCH (23 X 36 CM) FLATBREAD ⌁

The red onion on this flatbread provides just the right amount of
bite to cut through the barbecue flavor and really make
this combo sing.

Bench flour
(page 10)

1 prepared New
York–Style Dough
(Quick Version,
page 32)

Light olive oil, for
working the dough

1 cup (115 g)
Shredded Chicken
(page 173)

¼ cup (55 g)
Barbecue Sauce
(page 173)

¼ red onion, thinly
sliced

1 tablespoon extra
virgin olive oil

2 tablespoons
chopped fresh
cilantro

1. Set your oven rack in the middle position and place your baking steel on it. Preheat the oven to 550°F (285°C) for at least 1 hour.

2. While the oven is preheating, shape the dough: Place a 15-inch (38 cm) square piece of parchment paper on a flat surface. Dust about 1 tablespoon bench flour onto the parchment.

3. Using a spatula, scrape the dough out of the bowl onto the center of the parchment.

4. Generously coat the palms of your hands with light olive oil and gently press the dough into a uniformly thick 9 x 14-inch (23 x 36 cm) oval. Allow to rise for 20 minutes.

5. While the dough is rising, toss the Shredded Chicken and Barbecue Sauce in a small bowl to coat.

6. To finish the flatbread, distribute the chicken and onion over the surface of the risen dough.

7. Use a lightly floured pizza peel to launch the flatbread-on-parchment onto the baking steel in the oven. Bake for 2 minutes.

8. Strip the parchment (page 22). Bake for 6 to 7 minutes with the flatbread directly on the steel.

9. Remove the flatbread from the oven and transfer to a large cutting board. Top with the extra virgin olive oil and cilantro. Let set for 2 minutes, then slice and serve hot.

Shredded Chicken

MAKES 2 CUPS (250 G)

6 chicken drumsticks or 4 bone-in, skin-on chicken thighs

1 tablespoon olive oil

1 teaspoon garlic powder

1 teaspoon paprika

½ teaspoon salt

¼ teaspoon ground black pepper

1. Preheat the oven to 400°F (205°C).

2. Place the chicken in a bowl and drizzle with the oil, then add the remaining ingredients and toss to evenly coat. Place the chicken onto a baking sheet so the pieces are not touching.

3. Bake for 35 to 40 minutes, until a meat thermometer inserted into the center of the largest piece reads 165°F (75°C); juices should run clear and the meat should no longer be pink inside.

4. Remove from the oven and allow to cool. Remove the skin and shred the meat. If making ahead of time, let cool and store in an airtight container in the refrigerator for up to one week.

Barbecue Sauce

MAKES 1½ CUPS (430 G)

½ cup (142 g) ketchup

½ cup (125 g) puréed canned tomatoes

3 tablespoons packed brown sugar

2 tablespoons molasses

2 tablespoons apple cider vinegar

2 tablespoons Worcestershire sauce

1 tablespoon Dijon mustard

2 teaspoons hot sauce

½ teaspoon garlic powder

½ teaspoon onion powder

¼ teaspoon chili powder

¼ teaspoon paprika

¼ teaspoon salt

¼ teaspoon ground black pepper

1. Combine all of the ingredients in a saucepan. Bring to a boil, stirring constantly, then decrease the heat to medium-low and simmer for 5 minutes.

2. Remove from the heat and allow to cool. Store in an airtight container in the refrigerator for up to 3 weeks.

Fig and Prosciutto Flatbread

⤳ MAKES ONE 9 X 14-INCH (23 X 36 CM) FLATBREAD ⤳

Fig, prosciutto, and a balsamic glaze provide a perfect balance of salty sweetness on this popular flatbread.

Bench flour (page 10)

1 prepared New York–Style Dough (Quick Version, page 32)

Light olive oil, for working the dough

2 ounces (55 g) goat cheese, crumbled

1 ounce (30 g) thinly sliced prosciutto

3 tablespoons fig spread

8 fresh basil leaves, chiffonade

1 tablespoon Balsamic Glaze (page 131)

1 tablespoon extra virgin olive oil

1. Set your oven rack in the middle position and place your baking steel on it. Preheat the oven to 550°F (285°C) for at least 1 hour.

2. While the oven is preheating, shape the dough: Place a 15-inch (38 cm) square piece of parchment paper on a flat surface. Dust about 1 tablespoon bench flour onto the parchment.

3. Using a spatula, scrape the dough out of the bowl onto the center of the parchment.

4. Generously coat the palms of your hands with light olive oil and gently press the dough into a uniformly thick 9 x 14-inch (23 x 36 cm) oval. Allow the dough to rise for 20 minutes.

5. To finish the flatbread, distribute the goat cheese over the risen dough. Tear the prosciutto into pieces and add on top, then dollop on small amounts of fig spread.

6. Use a lightly floured pizza peel to launch the flatbread-on-parchment onto the baking steel in the oven. Bake for 2 minutes.

7. Strip the parchment (page 22). Bake for 6 to 7 minutes with the flatbread directly on the steel.

8. Remove the flatbread from the oven and transfer to a large cutting board. Top with the basil and drizzle with the Balsamic Glaze and extra virgin olive oil. Let set for 2 minutes, then slice and serve hot.

BUCKWHEAT
PIZZA

Like the teff in our California-style pizza dough, buckwheat is a nutrient-rich grain that performs really well in gluten-free baking. It adds a darker color and delicious nutty flavor. This can be too strong for certain pizza styles, such as New York, but paired with bold and/or spicy flavors, buckwheat can be a gluten-free pizza rock star.

Buckwheat Dough

⤳ MAKES ONE 12-INCH (30 CM) PIZZA ⤳

Buckwheat is a common ingredient for gluten-free pizzas in northern and eastern Europe, including Germany, where you can find *buchweizen* pizza on pizzeria menus. During Peter's business-travels to Berlin, he scoped out a number of pizzerias that offer gluten-free buckwheat crusts. Some use 100 percent buckwheat, but he prefers the approach of the pizzeria Cielo di Berlino, where they blend the buckwheat with other gluten-free flours—as we do here, too.

157 grams warm water (110°F/45°C)

1½ teaspoons sugar

1 teaspoon active dry yeast

50 grams brown rice flour

50 grams cornstarch

50 grams tapioca starch

30 grams buckwheat flour

1 teaspoon ground psyllium husk

¾ teaspoon salt

¼ teaspoon xanthan gum

1 tablespoon olive oil

High-altitude modification: Increase the water to 175 grams.

1. In a small bowl, whisk together the water, sugar, and yeast. Set aside to allow the yeast to activate, about 5 minutes, until foamy.

2. In a medium bowl, whisk together the rice flour, cornstarch, tapioca starch, buckwheat flour, psyllium husk, salt, and xanthan gum.

3. When the yeast mixture is foamy on top, add the oil and stir to combine.

4. Pour the yeast mixture into the flour mixture and stir vigorously with a spoon until it is smooth, there are no lumps, and it forms a wet dough.

Berliner

With bratwurst and knockwurst, this recipe goes all-in on classically German flavors.

1 teaspoon olive oil, plus more for working the dough and finishing the pizza

2 ounces (55 g) bratwurst, casings removed

Bench flour (page 10)

1 prepared Buckwheat Dough (page 179)

½ cup (115 g) puréed canned San Marzano tomatoes

⅛ teaspoon garlic powder

4 ounces (115 g) shredded low-moisture mozzarella

2 ounces (55 g) knockwurst, sliced

1. Set your oven rack in the middle position and place your baking steel on it. Preheat the oven to 550°F (285°C) for at least 1 hour.

2. While the oven is preheating, heat the oil in a large sauté pan over medium-high heat. Add the bratwurst. Sauté until cooked through, about 5 minutes. Set aside.

3. To shape the dough, place a 15-inch (38 cm) square piece of parchment paper on a flat surface. Dust about 1 tablespoon bench flour onto the parchment.

4. Using a spatula, scrape the dough out of the bowl onto the center of the parchment.

5. With oiled hands, gently press the dough into a 12-inch (30 cm) circle, leaving a small lip of raised dough around the perimeter edge (see page 19 for technique tips).

6. To finish the pizza, spread the tomatoes over the crust up to the raised edge. Sprinkle the garlic powder on top. Spread the mozzarella evenly over the sauce. Evenly distribute the bratwurst and knockwurst over the mozzarella.

7. Use a lightly floured pizza peel to launch the pizza-on-parchment onto the baking steel in the oven. Bake for 2 minutes.

8. Strip the parchment (page 22). Bake for 4 to 5 minutes with the pizza directly on the steel.

9. Remove the pizza from the oven and transfer to a large cutting board. Let set for 2 minutes, then slice and serve hot.

BACKCOUNTRY
PIZZA

Benjamin Franklin famously said that nothing in life is certain except death and taxes. In our family, we'd also add to that list our Sunday night gluten-free pizza tradition. The steady cadence of our weekly pizzas continues, even when we're camping in the wilderness of Colorado's Rocky Mountains and beyond.

We've made gluten-free pizzas on the shores of tiny alpine lakes, hidden in stands of evergreen trees at 11,000 feet above sea level, and perched on the edge of desert canyons—with nothing more than the ingredients, a small stove, and fuel we carried on our backs over miles of trail.

Whether you're backpacking into the backcountry or car camping around a fire ring at a campground, we have a method that will allow you to make pizza, no matter the circumstance, whether over a campfire, using a larger camp stove, or even a tiny backpacking stove.

Backcountry Pizzas

∾ MAKES THREE 7-INCH (18 CM) PIZZAS ∾

These pizzas—or, more accurately, their ingredients—are made to travel. The dough is based on our New York–Style Quick Version recipe (page 32), but instead of preparing a ball of dough at home, prep your ingredients prior to your camping trip.

1 recipe New York–Style Dough (Quick Version, page 32), prepared fresh at your campsite

Olive oil, for greasing and working the dough

¾ cup (170 g) New York–Style Tomato Sauce (page 35) or puréed canned San Marzano tomatoes

6 ounces (170 g) shredded or sliced low-moisture mozzarella

1 teaspoon dried basil

1 teaspoon dried oregano

1. **Before leaving home, prep the dough ingredients:** Pack the yeast and sugar in separate containers, as well as a small bottle of olive oil. Mix together the dry ingredients for the dough and store in a small container with a lid. (This container will double as your dough-mixing bowl once at your campsite.)

2. **At the campsite,** turn your camp stove on medium or build a fire in a ring with a cooking grate. Add a thin layer of oil to your camp pan/skillet.

3. **To make the dough,** combine warm water with the sugar and yeast in a bowl or backpacking pot. Set aside until the yeast is foamy. Add the oil and the flour mix. Stir until smooth.

4. Add a third of the dough to the pan. Oil your hands and press the dough out directly in the pan into a 7-inch (18 cm) circle with even thickness. (If your camp pan/skillet is larger or smaller, increase or decrease the amount of dough accordingly, making fewer or more pizzas than our recipe calls for.)

5. **To finish the pizza,** cook the dough over medium heat, keeping an eye on the bottom to make sure it doesn't burn. Cook until golden brown on the bottom, then flip.

6. Add a third of the sauce, mozzarella, and herbs. Place a piece of aluminum foil over the pan and return to the heat. Cook until the bottom of the crust is completely golden, with some charred spots, and the cheese is melted. (Depending upon your stove/fire and the weather, you will need to adjust where your pan is and the level of heat to make sure the crust is cooked through and not burned.)

7. Remove the pizza from the pan, allow to cool for 2 minutes, then cut and serve.

8. Repeat the process for the remaining two pizzas. Be careful pressing the subsequent crusts into the hot skillet (or allow the skillet to cool between pizzas).

Note: If you want to add toppings, such as pepperoni, cook them in your pan first, then set aside. Top the pizza with your parcooked toppings at the same time you add the sauce and cheese. (Because a backcountry pizza doesn't benefit from high oven temperatures, the toppings appreciate the precook!)

BREAKFAST

PIZZAS

Cold, leftover cheese pizza for breakfast is one thing. (We mean no disrespect, college students!) But proper breakfast pizza is quite another. With bacon and eggs, and toppings inspired by quiche and New York bagels, these breakfast pizzas are a great way to start your day . . . and proof that pizza really might be the most versatile food on the face of Earth!

Bacon, Egg, and Cheese

⌒ MAKES ONE 12-INCH (30 CM) PIZZA ⌒

Whether you prefer your bacon, egg, and cheese as an omelet, on a bagel, or on a piece of toast, you'll love it on a breakfast pizza. Feel free to substitute ham for the bacon and/or omit the cheese, with equally good results.

1 teaspoon olive oil, plus more for working the dough

8 slices bacon, crumbled, or ½ cup (115 g) diced ham

8 eggs

¼ cup (60 ml) milk

⅛ teaspoon salt

⅛ teaspoon ground black pepper

Bench flour (page 10)

1 prepared New York–Style Dough (Quick Version, page 32)

4 ounces (115 g) shredded cheddar

1. Set your oven rack in the middle position and place your baking steel on it. Preheat the oven to 550°F (285°C) for at least 1 hour.

2. While the oven is preheating, heat the oil in a large sauté pan over medium-high heat. Add the bacon. Cook until crispy, remove from the pan, and place on a paper towel to drain. Remove all but 1 tablespoon of the grease from the skillet and remove from the heat. (If you are making the pizza with ham, add 1 tablespoon oil to the pan instead of bacon grease.)

3. To shape the dough, place a 15-inch (38 cm) square piece of parchment paper on a flat surface. Dust about 1 tablespoon bench flour onto the parchment.

4. Using a spatula, scrape the dough out of the bowl onto the center of the parchment.

5. With oiled hands, gently press the dough into a 12-inch (30 cm) circle, leaving a small lip of raised dough around the perimeter edge (see page 19 for technique tips).

6. Return the skillet with reserved bacon grease to medium-high heat. In a medium bowl, whisk together the eggs, milk, salt, and pepper. Add the eggs to the hot skillet and cook until you have a soft scramble. Remove from the heat and set aside.

7. To finish the pizza, top the dough with the softly scrambled eggs, then bacon, and finally cheddar.

8. Use a lightly floured pizza peel to launch the pizza-on-parchment onto the baking steel in the oven. Bake for 2 minutes.

9. Strip the parchment (page 22). Bake for 6 to 7 minutes with the pizza directly on the steel.

10. Remove the pizza from the oven and transfer to a large cutting board. Let set for 2 minutes, then slice and serve hot.

Veggie Breakfast Pizza

⌁ MAKES ONE 12-INCH (30 CM) PIZZA ⌁

If you prefer meatless mornings, this veggie-packed breakfast pizza will start your day right.

1 tablespoon olive oil, plus more for working the dough

½ small yellow onion, thinly sliced

½ green bell pepper, thinly sliced

¼ teaspoon salt

¼ teaspoon ground black pepper

8 eggs

¼ cup (60 ml) milk

Bench flour (page 10)

1 prepared New York–Style Dough (Quick Version, page 32)

10 grape tomatoes, halved

4 ounces (115 g) shredded cheddar

1. Set your oven rack in the middle position and place your baking steel on it. Preheat the oven to 550°F (285°C) for at least 1 hour.

2. While the oven is preheating, heat the oil in a large sauté pan over medium heat. Add the onion and red pepper, season with ⅛ teaspoon each of the salt and pepper, and sauté until soft, about 5 minutes. Remove the vegetables from the pan and set aside.

3. To shape the dough, place a 15-inch (38 cm) square piece of parchment paper on a flat surface. Dust about 1 tablespoon bench flour onto the parchment.

4. Using a spatula, scrape the dough out of the bowl onto the center of the parchment.

5. With oiled hands, gently press the dough into a 12-inch (30 cm) circle, leaving a small lip of raised dough around the perimeter edge (see page 19 for technique tips).

6. Return the pan to medium-high heat, adding additional oil if the pan is too dry. In a medium bowl, whisk together the eggs, milk, and remaining salt and pepper. Add the eggs to the hot skillet and cook until you have a soft scramble.

Return the vegetables to the pan and toss to combine. Remove from the heat and set aside.

7. To finish the pizza, top the prepared crust with the eggs and vegetables, then the tomatoes, and finally the cheddar.

8. Use a lightly floured pizza peel to launch the pizza-on-parchment onto the baking steel in the oven. Bake for 2 minutes.

9. Strip the parchment (page 22). Bake for 6 to 7 minutes with the pizza directly on the steel.

10. Remove the pizza from the oven and transfer to a large cutting board. Let set for 2 minutes, then slice and serve hot.

Lox and Cream Cheese Pizza

≈ MAKES ONE 11 X 14-INCH (28 X 36 CM) PIZZA ≈

This pizza is unabashedly inspired by a Long Island bagel topped with a schmear of cream cheese and fresh lox. We've upgraded the breakfast-pizza version, adding herbs to the cream cheese spread, plus capers, sliced avocado, and some arugula, dressed in an easy lemon vinaigrette, alongside cold-smoked salmon.

4 ounces (115 g) cream cheese

3 tablespoons heavy cream

1 garlic clove, minced

1 green onion, minced

1 tablespoon minced dill

⅛ teaspoon salt

⅛ teaspoon ground black pepper

1 prepared Roman Cracker Dough (Quick Version, page 66)

Bench flour (page 10)

1½ tablespoons light olive oil

1 tablespoon nonpareil capers

3 ounces (85 g) thinly sliced cold-smoked salmon

½ avocado, sliced

1 teaspoon lemon juice

1 tablespoon extra virgin olive oil

1 small handful baby arugula

1. Set your oven rack in the middle position and place your baking steel on it. Preheat the oven to 550°F (285°C) for at least 1 hour.

2. While the oven is preheating, combine the cream cheese, heavy cream, garlic, green onion, dill, salt, and pepper in a small bowl and mix until smooth.

3. To shape the dough, place an unfloured 15-inch (38 cm) square piece of parchment paper on a flat surface.

4. Using a spatula, scrape the dough onto the center of the parchment. With floured hands, press the dough into a flattened rectangle.

5. Dust the surface of the dough and a rolling pin with bench flour. Roll the dough into a thin 11 x 14-inch (28 x 36 cm) rectangle (about ⅛ inch/ 3 mm thick), adding flour as needed to prevent sticking (see page 21 for technique tips).

6. Use a pizza wheel or sharp knife to trim away any jagged, uneven edges, leaving a smooth, finished edge with slightly rounded corners.

7. To bake the crust, brush the top of the dough with the 1½ tablespoons light olive oil from edge to edge. Use a lightly floured pizza peel to launch the dough-on-parchment onto the baking steel in the oven. Bake for 2 minutes.

8. Strip the parchment (page 22). Bake for 2 to 3 minutes with the crust directly on the steel, until the edges of the crust and the tops of the air pockets are golden brown.

9. Remove the crust from the oven and transfer to a large wire rack.

10. To finish the pizza, spread the herbed cream cheese over the crust. Top with the capers, salmon, and avocado.

11. In a small bowl, combine the lemon juice and extra virgin olive oil and toss the arugula to coat. Add the arugula to the pizza, then cut and serve.

Note: Our favorite salmon in this recipe—which has the added benefit of making your life easier when prepping the pizza—is Scottish-style salmon, sold thinly sliced and already interleaved.

DESSERT
PIZZAS

There's no reason to restrict pizzas to savory meals. These dessert pizzas indulge the sweeter side of life. If you can do a slice of cake for dessert, why not a slice of dessert pizza for, well, dessert?

Each recipe can be made into one 12-inch (30 cm) pizza or three smaller 7-inch (18 cm) pizzas. Simply press each small pizza onto an 8-inch (20 cm) piece of parchment and cook the same way as the large pizzas.

Frangipane

꩜ MAKES ONE 12-INCH (30 CM) PIZZA ꩜

It is no small secret that Kelli's favorite flavor is almond. We couldn't possibly publish a cookbook—including one dedicated to pizza—without at least one recipe in which almond is the centerpiece. This is it.

Bench flour (page 10)

1 prepared New York–Style Dough (Quick Version, page 32)

Olive oil, for working the dough

8 ounces (225 g) gluten-free almond paste

¼ cup (55 g) sugar

2 tablespoons (30 g) butter

2 eggs

2 tablespoons Chocolate Ganache (page 199)

3 ounces (85 g/½ cup) fresh raspberries

1. Set your oven rack in the middle position and place your baking steel on it. Preheat the oven to 550°F (285°C) for at least 1 hour.

2. While the oven is preheating, shape the dough: Place a 15-inch (38 cm) square piece of parchment paper on a flat surface. Dust about 1 tablespoon bench flour onto the parchment.

3. Using a spatula, scrape the dough out of the bowl onto the center of the parchment.

4. With oiled hands, gently press the dough into a 12-inch (30 cm) circle, leaving a small lip of raised dough around the perimeter edge (see page 19 for technique tips). Allow the dough to rise for 20 minutes.

5. While the dough is rising, using a stand or handheld mixer, combine the almond paste, sugar, and butter. Add the eggs and mix until smooth.

6. To finish the pizza, spread the almond mixture over the dough to the raised edge.

7. Use a lightly floured pizza peel to launch the pizza-on-parchment onto the baking steel in the oven. Bake for 2 minutes.

8. Strip the parchment (page 22). Bake for 6 to 7 minutes with the pizza directly on the steel.

9. Remove the pizza from the oven and allow to cool on a wire rack for about 5 minutes.

10. Drizzle with the Chocolate Ganache, and top with raspberries. Then cut and serve warm.

Chocolate-Hazelnut

⚬ MAKES ONE 12-INCH (30 CM) PIZZA ⚬

Our visit to Pizzeria Focacceria Quattrocento in quaint Marzana, north of Verona, Italy, was a leisurely, multicourse affair, with pizza after pizza. The feast concluded with a chocolate-hazelnut dessert pizza. From that moment, we knew we had to include our own take in this cookbook.

Bench flour (page 10)

1 prepared New York–Style Dough (Quick Version, page 32)

Olive oil, for working the dough

4 tablespoons chocolate-hazelnut spread

2 tablespoons Chocolate Ganache (page 199)

¼ cup chopped hazelnuts

Powdered sugar

1. Set your oven rack in the middle position and place your baking steel on it. Preheat the oven to 550°F (285°C) for at least 1 hour.

2. To shape the dough, place a 15-inch (38 cm) square piece of parchment paper on a flat surface. Dust about 1 tablespoon bench flour onto the parchment.

3. Using a spatula, scrape the dough out of the bowl onto the center of the parchment.

4. With oiled hands, gently press the dough into a 12-inch (30 cm) circle, leaving a small lip of raised dough around the perimeter edge (see page 19 for technique tips). Allow the dough to rise for 20 minutes.

5. To bake the crust, use a lightly floured pizza peel to launch the dough-on-parchment onto the baking steel in the oven. Bake for 2 minutes.

6. Strip the parchment (page 22). Bake for 4 to 5 minutes with the crust directly on the steel.

7. Remove the crust from the oven and allow to cool on a wire rack for about 5 minutes. While the crust is cooling, prepare the Chocolate Ganache.

8. To finish the pizza, spread the chocolate-hazelnut spread onto the crust, drizzle with the Chocolate Ganache, top with chopped hazelnuts, and finish with a generous dusting of powdered sugar. Cut and serve warm.

Chocolate Ganache

MAKES ¾ CUP (225 G)

½ cup (120 ml)
heavy cream

4 ounces (115 g/
about ⅔ cup)
bittersweet
chocolate

1. Bring the heavy cream to a simmer in a small saucepan over medium heat, then remove from the heat. Or microwave in a small glass bowl until the cream is hot.

2. Place the chocolate in a small bowl or glass jar. Carefully pour the hot cream over the chocolate and allow to sit for about one minute to soften the chocolate.

3. Stir until the chocolate is completely melted and the ganache is shiny and smooth. Use while the ganache is still warm.

Note: If the ganache is too thick, add a little additional cream. If the ganache cools and becomes too firm, gently reheat by placing the bowl/jar in a larger bowl of hot water, and stir until the desired consistency is reached; or gently microwave the ganache to re-warm. The recipe makes more ganache than the pizza needs, to allow for easier drizzling.

Caramelized Banana

ᔥ MAKES ONE 12-INCH (30 CM) PIZZA ᔥ

This dessert pizza is evocative of bananas Foster. If, like us, you perpetually have bananas on your kitchen counter threatening to overripen, put them to good use in this recipe.

Bench flour (page 10)

1 prepared New York–Style Dough (Quick Version, page 32)

Olive oil, for working the dough

4 tablespoons (60 g) butter

¼ cup (50 g) packed brown sugar

¼ teaspoon ground cinnamon

2 tablespoons orange juice

2 tablespoons brandy

2 bananas, peeled and sliced

½ cup (120 ml) heavy cream

1½ teaspoons granulated sugar

½ teaspoon gluten-free pure vanilla extract

1. Set your oven rack in the middle position and place your baking steel on it. Preheat the oven to 550°F (285°C) for at least 1 hour.

2. While the oven is preheating, shape the dough: Place a 15-inch (38 cm) square piece of parchment paper on a flat surface. Dust about 1 tablespoon bench flour onto the parchment.

3. Using a spatula, scrape the dough out of the bowl onto the center of the parchment.

4. With oiled hands, gently press the dough into a 12-inch (30 cm) circle, leaving a small lip of raised dough around the perimeter edge (see page 19 for technique tips). Allow the dough to rise for 20 minutes.

5. While the dough is rising, melt the butter in a sauté pan over medium heat. Add the brown sugar and stir. Add the cinnamon, orange juice, and brandy and stir. Add the bananas and simmer for 5 to 10 minutes, until the mixture is reduced by about 25 percent and syrupy. Remove from the heat and set aside.

6. To make the whipped cream: In a small bowl, combine the cream, sugar, and vanilla. Mix with a handheld mixer until soft peaks form, then set aside.

7. To finish the pizza, use a lightly floured pizza peel to launch the dough-on-parchment onto the baking steel in the oven. Bake for 2 minutes.

8. Strip the parchment (page 22). Bake for 4 to 5 minutes with the crust directly on the steel.

9. Remove the crust from the oven and spread the banana topping over the surface.

10. Top the center with a dollop of the whipped cream. Then slice and serve warm.

Ricotta and Berry Pizza

〜 MAKES ONE 12-INCH (30 CM) PIZZA 〜

Sweetened ricotta is a classic filling for Sicilian cannoli. But paired with fresh berries, it also makes a great topping for dessert pizza.

Bench flour (page 10)

1 prepared New York-Style Dough (Quick Version, page 32)

Olive oil, for working the dough

1 cup (225 g) Ricotta (see right)

1 tablespoon sugar

1 teaspoon gluten-free pure vanilla extract

12 ounces (340 g/ 2 cups) fresh berries (sliced if strawberries)

1 tablespoon honey

1. Set your oven rack in the middle position and place your baking steel on it. Preheat the oven to 550°F (285°C) for at least 1 hour.

2. **While the oven is preheating, shape the dough:** Place a 15-inch (38 cm) square piece of parchment paper on a flat surface. Dust about 1 tablespoon bench flour onto the parchment.

3. Using a spatula, scrape the dough out of the bowl onto the center of the parchment.

4. With oiled hands, gently press the dough into a 12-inch (30 cm) circle, leaving a small lip of raised dough around the perimeter edge (see page 19 for technique tips). Allow the dough to rise for 20 minutes.

5. **While the dough is rising,** mix together the Ricotta, sugar, and vanilla in a small bowl. Set aside.

6. **To finish the pizza,** use a lightly floured pizza peel to launch the dough-on-parchment onto the baking steel in the oven. Bake for 2 minutes.

7. Strip the parchment (page 22). Bake for 4 to 5 minutes with the crust directly on the steel.

8. Remove the crust from the oven and allow to cool for 5 minutes.

9. Spread the Ricotta on top of the crust. Decorate with the berries.

10. Put the honey in a microwave-safe bowl and warm, about 10 seconds. Drizzle over the pizza. Then slice and serve.

Ricotta

MAKES 1 CUP (225 G)

4 cups (960 ml) milk

½ cup (120 ml) heavy cream

½ teaspoon salt

1½ tablespoons lemon juice or distilled white vinegar

1. Set a colander or fine mesh strainer over a large bowl. Line with a double piece of cheesecloth, nut milk bag, or thin kitchen towel.

2. Pour the milk and cream into a large saucepan. Stir in the salt. Bring to a simmer over medium heat, stirring occasionally. Stir in the lemon juice and continue to simmer for 1 to 2 minutes, until the mixture curdles.

3. Pour into the prepared colander and allow to drain into the bowl for about 15 minutes.

4. Transfer the Ricotta to a separate container and use immediately or cover and refrigerate for up to 1 week. Discard the whey (the liquid in the bowl).

Fruit Tart Pizza

∽ MAKES ONE 12-INCH (30 CM) PIZZA ∾

Who says you need a pastry shell to enjoy a fruit tart?

1 cup (240 ml) milk

¼ cup (50 g) sugar

2 tablespoons cornstarch

2 large egg yolks

1 tablespoon (15 g) butter

1 teaspoon gluten-free pure vanilla extract

Bench flour (page 10)

1 prepared New York–Style Dough (Quick Version, page 32)

Olive oil, for working the dough

Fresh fruit (e.g., sliced strawberries, blueberries, raspberries, kiwi, mandarin orange segments)

¼ cup (80 g) apple or apricot jelly

1. Set your oven rack in the lower-middle position and place your baking steel on it. Preheat the oven to 550°F (285°C) for at least 1 hour.

2. While the oven is preheating, heat the milk in a saucepan over medium-high heat to bring to a simmer. Remove from the heat.

3. In a small bowl, whisk together the sugar and cornstarch. Add the egg yolks and whisk vigorously until the mixture loosens and turns a pale yellow color.

4. Temper the egg yolk mixture by slowly pouring half of the hot milk into the eggs while vigorously whisking. Continue whisking and pour the warmed egg yolks into the remaining milk in the saucepan. Return to the heat and bring to a boil, stirring constantly. Boil for 1 minute.

5. Remove from the heat and stir in the butter and vanilla. Transfer to a separate container and cover. Refrigerate until ready to use.

6. To shape the dough, place a 15-inch (38 cm) square piece of parchment paper on a flat surface. Dust about 1 tablespoon bench flour onto the parchment.

7. Using a spatula, scrape the dough out of the bowl onto the center of the parchment.

8. With oiled hands, gently press the dough into a 12-inch (30 cm) circle, leaving a small lip of raised dough around the perimeter edge (see page 19 for technique tips). Allow the dough to rise for 20 minutes.

9. To finish the pizza, use a lightly floured pizza peel to launch the dough-on-parchment onto the baking steel in the oven. Bake for 2 minutes.

10. Strip the parchment (page 22). Bake for 4 to 5 minutes with the crust directly on the steel.

11. Remove the crust from the oven and allow to cool for 5 minutes.

12. Remove the pastry cream from the refrigerator and whisk until very smooth, then spread it onto the cooled crust. Top with the fruit.

13. Put the jelly and 1 tablespoon water into a microwave-safe bowl. Heat for 10 to 20 seconds, until warm. Mix until smooth. Use a pastry brush to glaze the fruit until the entire surface is shiny. Cut and serve.

Acknowledgments

More than any cookbook we've written, this owes a debt of gratitude to *many* people. It would not have been possible without your support, your help, your insights, and your suggestions. Thank you!

First and foremost, to you, our readers. From the beginning, we have worked to serve the gluten-free community through our recipes and cookbooks. These pizzas are for you.

To everyone at The Experiment, especially Matthew, Liana, Olivia, Beth, Jennifer, Karen, and Jeanne. It's hard to believe we've partnered with The Experiment for more than a decade now. We're thrilled to continue the relationship with this fourth cookbook together and, as ever, appreciate the close collaboration and your helpful guidance that brings out the best in our cookbooks.

To food photographer extraordinaire Jennifer Olson, food stylist Eric Leskovar, and lighting guru David Budd for bringing these pizzas to life in wonderful images.

To our agent, Jenni Ferrari-Adler at Union Literary, for your ongoing support.

To our family, especially Kelli's parents, Bob and Linda Terry, and Peter's aunt and uncle, Flo and Joe Spirio, for letting us utterly take over your kitchens for sea-level recipe testing. And to our broader family as well, for lending us your taste buds, feedback, and flavor ideas.

To our friends at home in Colorado—or visiting us in Colorado from points afar—who endured an onslaught of pizzas for myriad taste-testing dinner parties, especially our Wednesday Night Dinner crew, the Airborne gymnastics families, the Niwot crew, Kelli's book club, and our neighbors.

To Lisa Etcheverry at SmackDaddy Pizza in Longmont, Colorado, for lending us your oven to practice in preparation for the 2018 Caputo Cup.

To Italian gluten-free blogger and fellow celiac and pizza-lover Valeria Torre, for sharing your passion for pizza and in-depth knowledge of Italy's gluten-free pizza scene with us.

To a long list of pizzaioli and pizzerias. You extended to us warm hospitality and an uncommonly gracious welcome into your kitchens to learn more about your ovens, your techniques, your ingredients, and your gluten-free pizza doughs. *Grazie mille.* Especially . . .

In northern Italy: brothers Bruno and Lorenzo Durizzi at Il Leone d'Oro in Telgate (Bergamo); Maria Laura, Roberto Fraschini, and Erika Masseretti at Ristorante Byron in Bergamo; the staff at Beato Te Milano in Milan; Nicoletta and the team at Ò Peperino e Milano in Milan; Besa, Fabrizio, and the team at Puglia Bakery & Bistrot in Milan; Federico De Silvestri, Mara Ruggieri, Mattia Melotti, and everyone at Pizzeria Focacceria Quattrocento in Marzana (Verona); and the staff at SG Lab in Forlì.

In and around Rome, Italy: the staff at Lievito 72; the staff at Rossopomodoro; the staff at Voglia di Pizza; Marcella and the team at Mama Eat in Trastevere (Rome); Douglas Barillaro and the team at Teresina Senza Glutine; and brothers Massimo and Stefano Di Michele at La Soffitta Renovatio.

In the Campania region in and around Naples, Italy: the staff at Umberto Ristorante Napoli; the staff at Mammina Pizzeria e Cucina Genuina; Don Antonio and the team at Starita; the staff at Pizzeria Vesi on Via Tribunali; father-daughter duo Angelo and Marina Caprio and the team at Ristorante e Pizzeria Mascagni; Roberto Susta and the team in Volla; Antonino Esposito and the team at Acqu'e Sale in Sorrento; the staff at Re Denari in Salerno; and pizzaiolo Antonio Langone.

In New York: Giovanni (John) Cesarano, his father, Ciro, and the team at King Umberto in Elmont; and father-daughter duo Roberto and Giorgia Caporuscio at Kesté Pizza & Vino.

And, of course, to our children: Marin, Charlotte, and Timothy. From flying halfway around the world with us for a tour-de-force of Italy's best gluten-free pizzas to happily eating more pizza in 2018 than most people will eat in a lifetime, your bottomless enthusiasm for gluten-free pizza has made this book a real joy. You're not just along for the ride—you're our copilots helping to navigate the journey. Here's to many more of our family's Sunday night pizzas together.

Index

NOTE: Page numbers in *italics* indicate a picture of the finished pizza. Page numbers in **bold** indicate a recipe in this cookbook that is used multiple times.

About the Authors

PETER AND KELLI BRONSKI are the husband-and-wife cofounders of the acclaimed blog No Gluten, No Problem and coauthors of the popular cookbooks *Artisanal Gluten-Free Cooking*, *Gluten-Free Family Favorites*, and *Artisanal Gluten-Free Cupcakes*. They've been developing recipes in their gluten-free kitchen since Peter's celiac disease diagnosis in 2007; they have a particular passion for pizza, which their family makes every Sunday night. Kelli is a graduate of Cornell University's prestigious School of Hotel Administration and a lifelong baker and cook. Peter is an award-winning writer and marketer, endurance athlete, and also the coauthor of *The Gluten-Free Edge*. They live in Colorado with their three children.

For more information, please visit them online: nogluten-noproblem.com.